AIN'T
IT TIME
WE SAID
GOODBYE

AIN'T IT TIME WE SAID GOODBYE

THE ROLLING STONES ON THE ROAD TO EXILE

ROBERT GREENFIELD

Da Capo Press

A Member of the Perseus Books Group

All rights reserved. No part of this publication may be reproduced, stored in a retrieval system, or transmitted, in any form or by any means, electronic, mechanical, photocopying, recording, or otherwise, without the prior written permission of the publisher. Printed in the United States of America. For information, address Da Capo Press, 44 Farnsworth Street, Third Floor, Boston, MA 02210.

Designed by Pauline Brown

Set in 10.5 point Sabon LT by The Perseus Books Group

Library of Congress Cataloging-in-Publication Data

Greenfield, Robert.

  Ain't it time we said goodbye : the Rolling Stones on the road to exile / by Robert Greenfield.

    pages cm

  Includes bibliographical references and index.

  ISBN 978-0-306-82312-1 (hardcover) — ISBN 978-0-306-82313-8 (e-book) 1. Rolling Stones. 2. Rock musicians—England—Biography. I. Title.

  ML421.R64G68 2014

  782.42166092'2—dc23

  [B]

                            2014002616

Published by Da Capo Press

A Member of the Perseus Books Group

www.dacapopress.com

Da Capo Press books are available at special discounts for bulk purchases in the U.S. by corporations, institutions, and other organizations. For more information, please contact the Special Markets Department at the Perseus Books Group, 2300 Chestnut Street, Suite 200, Philadelphia, PA 19103, or call (800) 810-4145, ext. 5000, or e-mail special.markets@perseusbooks .com.

10 9 8 7 6 5 4 3 2 1

FOR IAN STEWART,
who was the bravest of them all

Oh, who listens to Chuck Berry anymore?
I mean, I haven't listened to that stuff in years.
For God's sake, I listen to the MC5. Rock 'n' roll's
not over. I don't like to see one thing end until I see
another beginning. Like when you break up with a
woman. Do you know what I mean?
MICK JAGGER, MARCH 8, 1971

CONTENTS

BEFORE THE TRAIN LEFT THE STATION

NO ONE EVER FORGETS their first tour with the Rolling Stones. For those fortunate enough to have gone along for the ride and survived with enough brain cells still intact to tell the tale, it remains a life-changing experience of the first order. Although they did not know it then, when the Rolling Stones embarked on their farewell tour of Great Britain in March 1971 after having announced they were about to go into tax exile in the South of France, it was the end of an era. For the Stones, nothing would ever be the same again.

Once the band decamped to the South of France to record *Exile on Main St.*, the album now widely recognized as their masterpiece, all the subtle seeds of dissension and conflict that had been sown during the farewell tour suddenly burst into full, riotous bloom, with consequences that would prove disastrous for all concerned.

Forsaking their hard-earned legacy as the illegitimate sons of Chuck Berry, the Stones crossed over from the outlaw world of rock 'n' roll and became international superstars. When they went on the road in America during the summer of 1972 to play in huge arenas on what became the highest-grossing rock tour in history to that point in time, nothing was as it had been in England just fourteen months before.

As the only journalist who accompanied the band on their farewell tour of England, I was then just twenty-five years old and more or less straight out of Brooklyn by way of a hippie commune in California as well as a long, hot summer spent wandering aimlessly through Europe in search of true love, spiritual enlightenment, and some kind of a career as a writer. Returning to England at the end of August 1970 to attend the Isle of Wight Festival as a journalist, I then spent the next six months working in the London bureau of *Rolling Stone* magazine.

When the Stones announced they were about to go on tour, I came up with the bright idea of accompanying them to each and every gig. While I had never before seen the band perform and had no idea what I was going to write about them, I wanted to be able to observe the Stones at close range without making anyone aware of what I was doing. Never taking notes where people could see me do so, I instead spent a good deal of my time on the tour going to the bathroom so I could scribble down everything I had just seen and heard.

What I did not then know about the Rolling Stones was how practiced both Mick Jagger and Keith Richards already were at the art of deception. And so while I was having the time of my life riding to gigs in the back of long black limousines while partaking of whatever happened to be going around at the moment, a real-life rock 'n' roll soap opera of major proportions was unfolding right before my eyes.

For what both Mick Jagger and Keith Richards were truly saying farewell to on this tour was not just Great Britain but also the way in which they had related to one another to this point in time. Although the music they made together onstage during those ten days in March was absolutely brilliant and the future of the band seemed bright with rosy promise, their long-term friendship was about to finally fall apart, never to be repaired again.

///

Through all that follows, I will occasionally be jumping in with my hat in my hand in italics just like these to amplify and clarify what I have since learned was really happening between the buttons and under cover of night on that tour. For want of a better term, let's just call it a continuing conversation between the wide-eyed, twenty-five-year-old true believer in rock 'n' roll I was back then and the somewhat cranky and cynical senior citizen I now somehow seem to have become.

///

And now, without further ado, this is what it was like to be on tour with the Rolling Stones a long time ago in a galaxy that now seems very far, far away indeed. Enough said. See you on the road.

PART ONE

GOODBYE,

GREAT BRITAIN

CHAPTER ONE

NEWCASTLE, MARCH 4, 1971

IN THE EMPTY KING'S CROSS MAIN LINE STATION in North London on a cold, clear Thursday that feels like November in New York, the 12:00 train to Doncaster, York, Darlington, Newcastle, Dunbar, Edinburgh, and Aberdeen is leaving from track 8. Although the Rolling Stones are about to go off on tour in the land of their birth for the first time in five years, no screaming hordes of fans, nor a single reporter save for yours truly, have come to see them off.

In part, this is because from way back when Ian Stewart, their former piano player, was still driving them to gigs all over England in an old VW van, the Stones have always been a traveling band who go out on the road night after night to perform and then move on to do it all over again in another town. In part, it is also because what with the Beatles having only recently shocked their millions of fans by breaking up in the most contentious manner imaginable, the Stones have now become such an integral part of English culture that their comings and goings over here no longer attract the same kind of attention that had been lavished upon them in America since they first played at Carnegie Hall in New York in 1964.

Nonetheless, with all the necessary plans and preparations having been made and a brand-new album soon to be released on their very own record label, the Stones are about to set off on a ten-day journey through Newcastle, Manchester, Coventry, Glasgow, Bristol, Brighton, Liverpool, Leeds, and London that they have announced will serve as their farewell tour of their homeland.

The England they are about to leave to go into tax exile in the South of France bears very little resemblance to the England we now know. Even in London, a great city by any definition of the term, central heating is still an entirely foreign concept in 1971. To keep warm during the long winter months, most people feed sixpences into a coin-operated electric heater mounted on a wall while wearing as many layers of clothing as possible. For those who live in tiny bed-sitter flats in London, the loo is almost always down the stairs and the only shower may well be located in the basement where it is shared by all who live in the building.

As virtually no one I know in London owns a car, traffic is not an issue. Although the British pound is worth an astonishing $2.40, everything is still so cheap in England that anyone can sit like a lord in the back of a black cab while being driven from one end of London to the other for less than a quid and still have enough money left over to hand the driver a generous tip.

Since tiny garret flats like the one in which I live rent for as little as £6 (about $15) a week, those who earn the average weekly wage of £28 ($67) and do not have a family to support can easily afford to keep themselves in food and drink while still depositing more than half that sum in their bank account.

In England, there are only three television channels: BBC-1, BBC-2, and ITV. Those who watch them usually do so on a set they have acquired through "hire purchase," paying a nominal fee each month until the set finally becomes their own. Even in London, most people still prefer to spend their evenings drinking in local pubs, which promptly shut their doors at 11:00 PM. Since a pint of bitter costs just 11 pence (about 11 cents), most regulars have consumed their limit by the time "last call" is sounded.

Despite the fact that England has been the preeminent source of popular music in the world for the past decade, British radio is a vast and utter wasteland. Because there are no hip free-form FM stations and the pop songs played on BBC 1, 2, 3, and 4 are utterly bland and vapid, the preferred way to listen to music is to pass a three- or five-paper English hash joint from hand to hand as an album goes round on a turntable in someone's flat.

While this may seem impossible for those under the age of thirty to comprehend, there is no Internet. No email, no Facebook, no Twitter, and no YouTube. There are no cell phones. Some people in London do not even own a phone and so have to walk to a call box across the road with a pocket full of coins to contact whoever might be interested in talking to them.

Although the daily tabloid newspapers that traffic in celebrity gossip all have huge circulations, the straight press in England usually restricts their coverage of pop stars to headline stories about drug busts and sex scandals. And while the pop press has most definitely noted that the Rolling Stones are beginning what they have announced will be their farewell tour of Great Britain, no one has leaked the news of their departure from London today and so I am the only journalist who has come to see them off.

In the King's Cross Main Line station in this England that no longer exists, Nicky Hopkins, the brilliant rock 'n' roll pianist who went to California for a week and wound up staying there for two years as a member of Quicksilver Messenger Service, keeps hopping on and off the train to snap photographs of anything that looks typically English to him, like all the crumpled purple-and-white Cadbury chocolate wrappers that litter the platform.

As he does so, Charlie Watts comes walking toward the train accompanied by his father, who has spent his life working as a lorry driver for British Railways. Precisely why he is here, no one can say for sure, but as five to twelve becomes four, three, two, one, and a conductor with a green flag in his pocket comes down the line closing all the doors, Charlie's father says, "Awright, Charlie, awright now, I don't want to go, lemme off." Hopping off the train at the very last moment, Charlie's father disappears into a cloud of gray white steam that curls up from beneath the wheels of the train as it rolls out of London heading north.

While by all rights any account of the Rolling Stones on tour should begin with a detailed description of the whereabouts of Mick Jagger and Keith Richards, the two central figures of this tale, both of them, as well as guitarist Mick Taylor, have missed the train. Although the Stones cannot possibly go onstage tonight without them, no one seems particularly concerned about their absence. As it turns out, the two Micks will catch a later train and arrive in plenty of time for the show. Beginning a pattern of behavior that will persist throughout the entire tour, Keith misses that one as well and has to be driven up to Newcastle.

As pelting small-flake snow starts coming down outside the windows of the train, Nicky Hopkins just keeps right on snapping photographs of all the dark, satanic mills that have dotted this green and pleasant land ever since William Blake cried out for a bow of burning gold and the arrows of desire. A painfully thin man with dark hollows beneath his eyes, long hair that hangs down to his shoulders, and a droopy cowboy mustache, Nicky wears a fringed buckskin jacket that makes him look like a psychedelic gunslinger from Marin County. Thoroughly English in every way, he gazes wistfully out the window as the train speeds past an open field and says, "I love sheep. They just stand there and grow."

What I did not then know about Nicky Hopkins was how sick he had been ever since childhood. Then twenty-seven years old, he had already had much of his large intestine and one of his kidneys removed. Having first worked with the Stones on Between the Buttons *in 1966, Nicky had played on five tracks on* Beggars Banquet *as well as on "Sway" and "Can't You Hear Me Knocking" during the band's recent sessions for* Sticky Fingers.

Wherever he went for the next ten days, Hopkins was always accompanied by a woman whose name appears nowhere in my notebooks because everyone on the tour seemed to know her only as The Person Who Is In Charge of Nicky. A good-looking but intimidating presence with a pronounced New Jersey accent she did her best to hide by trying to sound English, she had long straight hair, brightly polished blood-red fingernails, and an attitude that can only be described as truly formidable.

Since her entire focus was on taking care of Nicky while also constantly telling him what to do, no one ever willingly engaged her in conversation or made any effort whatsoever to find out who she really was. At some point during the tour, someone mistakenly told me she had formerly been married to Al Kooper, yet another wildly gifted keyboard player who by then had become famous as the founder of Blood, Sweat, and Tears. As I later learned, this was not true.

Nicky seemed so gentle and sweet-tempered that it was impossible not to like him even though the woman he was with always treated him like an invalid, which he most definitely was not. Although the term was not then in vogue, the two of them were beyond codependent. Simply, it was a relationship that made you want to never be around them for very long, especially if you thought Nicky was something special, which I most certainly did. Seven months after the tour ended, the two would be married but as they say in the movies, that is another story altogether.

The real point about Nicky Hopkins on this tour was that with him on piano, an instrument that back then could never be miked well enough to hear all the impossibly liquid notes that flowed from his fingertips like water, the Stones were now able to go places in their music onstage where they had never been before.

Having taken LSD for the first time when he was dosed in the studio while recording Shady Grove with Quicksilver in 1969, Nicky Hopkins played piano in what I can still only describe as a truly psychedelic manner. And while I saw Nicky smoke the occasional joint and take a drink every now and then during the tour, his talent was so immense and his physical condition so frail that it seems impossible to me even now that shortly after becoming a Scientologist in 1986, Nicky Hopkins would estimate that he had spent a million pounds on alcohol, Valium, heroin, and pot.

Without a sound check and only a week of rehearsal, the Stones begin the tour in Newcastle, a gray, scruffy, soulful city on the banks of the Tyne that has lately fallen on hard times. In the sold-out City Hall, more than two thousand people, many of whom stood in line for as long as sixteen hours to buy tickets costing anywhere from fifty pence ($1.20) to a pound, wait patiently for the band to go onstage in England for the first time since they performed in London in December 1969.

Seen at close range before the show as he sits before a mirror putting cream on his face in a narrow dressing room with white walls, Mick Jagger, then just twenty-seven years old, looks oddly frail and very pale. Nervously bumping his toe against the floor by the dressing room door, Bobby Keys, the Stones' beefy, florid-faced sax player, says, "Let's do it. I'm ready. Yeah, I'm ready. Been ready for years."

Pointing to the room where Keith Richards and Mick Taylor sit behind a closed door, Charlie Watts, whose bag has been lost in transit but does not seem all that concerned about it because all he brought with him was a toothbrush, a handkerchief, and a pair of drumsticks, says, "They're tunin' up. They been fuckin' tunin' up for fifteen minutes. We should be on. What are they gonna do when things go wrong?"

Putting down the copy of Melody Maker he has been carefully perusing beneath the baleful gaze of a large English policeman, Mick Jagger says, "Hang on. We're comin'." Getting to his feet, he grabs Charlie by the shoulders, pushes him halfway out the door, and says, "Go on, Charlie. Go on."

In a pink sateen suit and a multicolored jockey's cap, Mick leads the band onstage and starts the set with "Jumpin' Jack

Flash." The Stones then go into "Live with Me," followed by "Dead Flowers," a song off their as yet unreleased new album. Far more intimidating than his songwriting partner in every way, Keith Richards sits down beside Mick on a wooden stool in a purple spotlight and picks out a dead-perfect acoustic version of Robert Johnson's "Love in Vain," followed by "Prodigal Son."

What has been a series of brilliantly played songs suddenly becomes something else again as the Stones go into "Midnight Rambler." As it will break down nightly on the tour, the song begins with anywhere from six to twelve bars of basic blues as Keith slings one guitar off over his head and gets another one on and tuned so he can launch into the song's driving riff. After Mick sings the first four verses, the psychodrama begins with just Bill Wyman's bass pulsing away and the lights going all blue and eerie on Mick's face.

Taking off the studded black belt he wears around his waist, Mick gets down on his knees and begins crooning, "Beggin' with ya, baby . . . go down on me, bay-bay, uh, uh." Rising to his feet in a slow and decidedly sinister manner, Mick wails, "Well, you heard about de Bos-ton. . . . " As he stretches out the second syllable, Mick dangles the belt behind his shoulder. Slashing the belt down onto the stage as the band comes back in behind him and all the lights go blood red in his face, Mick wails, "Honey, it's not one of those. . . . "

As one, the entire crowd lets out its collective breath. Young girls who have just gotten what this song is all about giggle nervously. With the band hitting everything in sight, Mick prowls the edge of the stage hunched over like an evil old man. After the song crashes to a shattering climax, the Stones go right into "Bitch," with Bobby Keys and trumpet player Jim Price blowing stomping circles against the melody.

Stepping to the microphone, Mick says, "And now, a song for all the whores in the audience." After the Stones tear through "Honky Tonk Women," they launch into a long, unrecognizable introduction that suddenly becomes "Satisfaction." Solidly crazed by what they are now hearing, the crowd in Newcastle starts rocking down the aisles. Middle-aged ladies in toreador pants who seem to have come straight out of 1957 bump obscenely to the beat as skinheads in Ben Sherman polo shirts, neatly pressed jeans, and black Doc Martens boots idiot-dance in the balcony.

Chuck Berry's "Little Queenie" is followed by "Brown Sugar" and then "Street Fighting Man." At its climax, Mick flings a wicker basket filled with yellow daffodils into the house. As the final chords of the song ring out through the hall and flower petals slowly come floating down through the spotlight beams, Mick leaps four feet into the air and screams.

To huge applause, the Rolling Stones exit stage right. In an hour and a half, they have done twelve songs. Despite how long and hard everyone goes right on cheering, that's it. The first show of the tour is over and as everyone who has traveled with the Stones before already knows, this is a band that does not do encores.

Between shows, the dressing room is oddly calm and very quiet. As Keith Richards jiggles his eighteen-month-old son Marlon up and down on his knee, bassist Bill Wyman says to no one in particular, "Do you remember carryin' an amp around Newcastle in a wheelbarrow?" With one more show to do tonight, people sit in small groups talking to one another while smoking Dunhill

International filter cigarettes that cost far too much for most of their fans to ever afford.

Although it does not seem possible, the second show is even better than the first. With a cigarette dangling from the corner of his mouth and two bottles of whiskey propped up before him on the piano, Nicky Hopkins only moves from the wrists down as he plays killer honky-tonk riffs. Corkscrewing his body in ever-tighter circles as he gets off on the music and his silver-studded earring swings into view for the first time, Keith turns his back on the house to seesaw back and forth into Charlie's big Gretsch bass drum.

With his jack-o'-lantern face turned to the side and his mouth open, Charlie doubles up and starts drumming against himself like a tightly wound metronome. Trooping off the stage once more after "Street Fighting Man" ends, the Stones head for the dressing room. Outside the hall, a line of long black limousines waits to take them to their hotel.

Wearing a blue nylon windbreaker that makes him look like he just shot eighteen holes on a local golf course, Ian Stewart walks into the dressing room and says, "Curtain call, chappies."

"They don't do curtain calls," their publicity person says.

Chip Monck, who is colloquially known as the "Voice of Woodstock," or just "VOW," on the tour and has been calling light cues all night long while dancing beside the piano, sticks his head in the door and says, "No one is leaving."

"Go out and play some songs on piano, Stu," Keith says.

"No one," Chip Monck repeats, "is leaving."

Slumped in a chair, Mick looks at Keith and says, "What do we do then? We should go quickly."

"What do we do?" Keith asks.

"Uh," Mick says, "'Peggy Sue'?"

"If we're going," Keith says. "Someone better tell them."

Pouring through a narrow door, the Stones walk back onstage into a cosmos of light and noise for their first encore in three years, "Sympathy for the Devil" followed by Chuck Berry's "Let It Rock." With the house lights all the way up as Keith chops the rhythm into half and quarter notes, the crowd has now become part of the show and everyone is on their feet and dancing as Mick bumps and grinds at the front of the stage like the second coming of a somewhat spastic James Brown.

Drinking Scotch whiskey from a white paper cup in the dressing room after the encore is over, Bobby Keys shouts out, "Chawlie! Chawlie Watts! What do you mean, stirrin' up all these people like that?"

"Naw, Bobby," Charlie says. "It was you. I saw you through the whole thing, just plottin' to make it happen."

///

In every sense back then, Bobby Keys considered himself a full-fledged member of the Rolling Stones. No shrinking violet he, Bobby's personality was so high-voltage that it could light up an entire auditorium. Unlike Jim Price, who rarely if ever spoke, or Mick Taylor, who on this tour still seemed incredibly shy and unsure of himself except when he was performing onstage, Bobby Keys was always perfectly happy to let fly with whatever came into his mind at any given moment without bothering to censor himself in any way whatsoever.

That the Stones in general and Mick Jagger in particular were willing to put up with Bobby Keys on a nightly basis spoke not just to how much they appreciated his skill as a musician but also to their very English tolerance and fondness for real characters who were never afraid to be themselves in their presence.

//

Because there is nowhere else to eat in Newcastle at this hour, a long table covered in white linen has been set for forty people in a ballroom at the Five Bridges Hotel in Gateshead, just across from Newcastle on the River Tyne. Forty clear glass tumblers, forty knives, forty forks, and forty spoons all sit perfectly aligned beside forty gleaming white plates. At two in the morning, the entire scene is a true beggars' banquet, not to mention a bit of surrealism, Rolling Stones style.

//

Despite what it says in my notebooks, this almost certainly cannot be right as there were only nineteen people on the tour. There was a road crew of twelve, half of them English and half of them American, but no one ever saw them because once the show was over, they were all busily breaking down the stage so they could load all the gear into a twenty-two-foot bobtail truck, also known as a "five-tonner" in England.

As everyone was sitting down to dinner in the hotel that night, the crew was still back at the hall. As Chip Monck would later say, "My favorite story of that whole tour was Newcastle City Hall with Mr. Brown, who came out after the second show was over with a loaf of bread, a paint pot, and a little brush. He said, 'Now, I'm terribly sorry to interrupt your load-out but I wondered if you could do me a favor? As this is a council hall, we try to keep it as best we can. Now, you've made some penetrations in the wall up there, so I wonder if you would just take this bread and stick it in the hole and wait for it to dry and perhaps before you leave, you could just paint over it?' And I said, 'Yes, Mr. Brown.'"

At the head of the table, a small man with dark hair, piercing eyes, and a beaked nose is working Mick for all he's worth. Having only just flown into London this morning from New York, Marshall Chess, whose father and uncle founded the legendary Chicago blues label bearing the family name, is the man whom Mick and Keith have chosen to run Rolling Stones Records. Intent on getting final approval from Mick so the new album can be released on time, Marshall is even more wired than usual tonight, which in his case is really saying something.

In a white linen cape and a wide-brimmed hat she wears pushed back on her head, Bianca Pérez-Mora Macias sits silently by Mick's side. Her face is so beautiful as to be insolent—high cheekbones, a cruel mouth, and features so sharp that Mick must sometimes feel like he is staring into a mirror whenever he looks at her. Whether she has any interest whatsoever in the subject currently under discussion is another question altogether.

"More than twenty minutes on a side and you lose level," Marshall says. "You know that. It's how they cut the grooves. So we have to work out the running order."

Further down the table, Jim Price asks Charlie Watts, "You dig Skinnay Ennis, the cat who blew that solo on 'We Meet and the Angels Sing'?"

A dyed-in-the-wool jazz fanatic from way back, Charlie says, "Fantastic."

Shrugging off the cloak of invisibility I donned when I boarded the train to Newcastle, I open my mouth for the first time on the tour and say, "That was Ziggy Elman."

"He's from my hometown," Jim Price says.

"Who?" Charlie asks.

"Skinnay Ennis," Price says.

"You mean Ziggy Elman, man?" I say.

Shaking his head sadly, Charlie says, "They're both dead."

"Henry Busse too," Price says. "On 'I Can't Get Started with You.'"

"Fantastic," Charlie says, making the word sound like a soft cymbal crash with brushes.

As I would later learn, Jim Price was born in Fort Worth, Texas, and then grew up in Midland, while Skinnay Ennis hailed from Salisbury, North Carolina. Since this was long before such facts could be checked on the Internet, I simply wrote down what I had heard and then reported it as the gospel truth. At three in the morning in Newcastle, what really mattered most, at least in my own mind, was that by coming up with Ziggy Elman's name on the spur of the moment, I had established my own credentials as someone worthy of traveling with the Stones.

Ignoring everything else that is going on around him, Marshall Chess leans in even closer to Mick and says, "I can send you a test pressing by air, and you can send me back a dub."

"By hand," Mick says.

"By air and hand," Marshall tells him. "And you send me back a dub."

"You'll send me one too," Charlie suddenly calls out.

A little surprised, Marshall says, "We will, Charlie."

Smiling, Charlie says, "Just addin' to the bravado."

"Will you do it that way, Mick?" Marshall implores. "Will you?"

In a voice made far louder by the fact that he is now in England, Bobby Keys says, "Ah'm gonna burn down this goddamn hotel if ah don't find mah suitcase. Goddamn, ah'll throw Charlie Watts out a window."

Spying a hapless waitress who just happens to be passing by with a serving platter in her hands, Keys says, "What's that? Slide one of them on mah plate, lady." Picking up the small dinner roll she has just given him, Keys says, "You know what these are good for?"

Already knowing what is about to happen, Jim Price softly says, "Oh-oh."

Whang, a dinner roll goes spinning through the air.

"You know what these glasses are good for?" Keys asks rhetorically.

Back up at the head of the table, Marshall asks, "Will you do it that way, Mick? Will you? If we cut 'Moonlight Mile' to four verses and make up a running order so the guy in the States can get started on the sleeves?"

Mumble, mumble. It's now four in the morning, and Mick has his head down talking to Bianca in a voice only she can hear. When he finally lifts his head, Mick looks more than a little glazed. From the completely blank expression on his face, it seems plain that he has not heard a single word Marshall Chess has said to him in the last ten minutes.

Having already done two shows tonight, Mick Jagger is now being asked to make a decision that will affect not only the release of the new album but the future of the band as well. Looking very much like an English schoolboy at the end of a very long and trying day, Mick says, "What, Marshall?"

CHAPTER TWO

MANCHESTER, MARCH 5, 1971

WHAT WITH ALL THE CHANGES the psychedelic revolution has wreaked upon the world, both Jimi Hendrix and Janis Joplin less than six months dead, and the counterculture they helped spawn in America now most definitely on life support as the war in Vietnam rages on, do people still politely approach stars like the Rolling Stones to ask for autographs? In Newcastle, where it sometimes seems like the Depression has never ended and the city still looks as it did back in the 1930s, they most certainly do.

As all those members of the band who have somehow managed to rouse themselves by midmorning sit at small tables in the hotel dining room eating breakfast, a steady stream of gray-haired little old ladies, Irish chambermaids, and middle-aged waitresses come up to offer them menus and tissues as well as any bit of paper on which they can lay their hands.

Fidgeting nervously from one foot to the other as they stand there waiting, they say, "Are you a Stone then? Will you sign this for me? Will you? I'd appreciate it ever so much." And because this is England, where everyone has been raised to always be as polite as humanly possible, the Stones dutifully do just as they are asked.

Although they were able to make their way out of London without attracting any undue media attention, the mere presence of the Rolling Stones here in Newcastle is most definitely news. Wearing a natty dark double-breasted blazer and an outrageous wide-brimmed hat, Mick strolls into the hotel lobby once breakfast is over only to be greeted by two very straight newspaper reporters, who immediately turn to a hipper-looking colleague and ask, "Is he one of them?"

///

While it may now seem difficult to believe that anyone could not recognize Mick Jagger in the flesh despite how long he had been famous in his native land, a reporter from the News of the World *made this very same mistake on February 5, 1967 by writing that after Mick had taken six amphetamine tablets while brandishing a lump of hashish in Blaise's nightclub in South Kensington, he openly acknowledged having first taken LSD while on the road with Bo Diddley and Little Richard, but "didn't go much on it now [that] the cats had taken it up. It'll just get a dirty name."*

No doubt so stoned out of his head at the time that it seemed like a good idea to send up the reporter in this manner, the Stone in question was actually Brian Jones, who always liked to refer to himself as "the original founder of the Rolling Stones." On The Eamonn Andrews Show *on Thames Television that night, Mick promptly announced he would be suing the newspaper for libel.*

A week later, the News of the World *helped engineer the drug bust at Redlands, Keith's country home in Sussex. The*

*draconian sentences meted out to Mick and Keith at the end of
a trial that was front-page news then made them both authentic
counterculture heroes in England. While so much had changed
over here since then, the British press still delighted in tearing
down those whom it had already made rich and famous and so
just as soon as Mick's identity was confirmed beyond any shadow
of a doubt, an impromptu media circus began with him standing
squarely in the center ring.*

Zip! Suddenly, the lobby is brilliantly flood-lit. As a camera-
man begins rolling film, an interviewer from the BBC steps forward with a microphone in his hand. Sticking it right into Mick's
face, the interviewer says, "A-hah, ahem, in his interview in *Rolling Stone* magazine, John Lennon said that what the Beatles did
yesterday, the Stones do tomorrow. Are you then too planning to
break up?"

Like a goofy teenager who thinks this is either the dumbest or
funniest thing he has ever heard, Mick's face cracks wide open as
he begins to laugh. "Naw, we're not breakin' up," he says. "And
if we did, we wouldn't be as bitchy about it as them." When the
interviewer asks why the Stones have now chosen to go live in
France, Mick says it was Keith's idea, which is most certainly not
the case.

Pursuing a line of inquiry that seems to make sense only to
him, the interviewer then asks, "Is the band tired?"

"Charlie!" Mick calls out. "Are you tired of all this then, the
one-night stands and all?" As Charlie is far too busy at the moment creeping around behind the cameras while asking everyone

who is being interviewed to respond, Mick says, "Naw, we started last night and we're just gonna go on until the body gives out."

Zip! Off go the floodlights. Shoving his hands into his jacket pockets, Mick heads out the front door where a photographer from the *Daily Mirror* begins snapping his every movement as he puts his bags into the boot of the white Bentley that will take him and Bianca to Manchester for tonight's two shows.

///

As I stood there watching them drive away, Jo Bergman appeared by my side. A short and bubbly woman with an outrageous mane of frizzy black hair and an infectious laugh, she had been brought over from America by Brian Epstein to help him run the Beatles' fan club. For the past four years, she had been in charge of the Stones' office at 46A Maddox Street in London. And so when she offered me a ride to Manchester, I happily accepted and clambered into the backseat of a rented Ford Cortina.

Only then did I realize that the man behind the wheel was Ian Stewart. Thirty-two years old, "Stu," as he was called by one and all, was short, square, and stocky, with piercing blue eyes, prematurely gray streaks in his hair, and a prognathous jaw that caused former manager Andrew Loog Oldham to decide he did not look enough like a Rolling Stone to continue playing piano with the band but should instead begin driving them to gigs.

While this particular job had long since been passed on to others, Stu still arrived at the hall long before every show so he could set up Charlie's drum kit and make sure everything onstage was exactly where it should be. By having never changed at all since he first met the band while auditioning for them in an upstairs room at the Bricklayer's Arms pub in Soho in 1962, Stu had become the only person whom the Stones trusted to always tell them the truth. On this tour, Stu would also occasionally slide behind the piano to play on songs that did not contain what he called "any Chinese chords."

Clad as always today in a blue nylon windbreaker and a pair of plain cloth pants that make him look for all the world like just another roadie, Stu begins negotiating his way out of the city. Turning to Jo Bergman, he points out the window and says, "See that grotty transport caf over there? We literally had to force them to turn on the TV in 1963 when we were on *Thank Your Lucky Stars* for the first time. We walked in there and everyone said, 'What? A bunch of longhairs like you on the telly?' And I can tell you this, that TV never worked properly either."

A cautious and canny Scot whose drug of choice is good malt whiskey, Stu definitely becomes someone else again when he gets behind the wheel of a car. Putting the accelerator all the way down to the floor as soon as we leave Newcastle, Stu begins driving like his namesake, the world champion Grand Prix racer Jackie Stewart. Going at what he would call "a vast rate of knots," Stu attacks each and every treacherous curve on the narrow winding road that leads through the towering range of hills known as the Pennines like he is trying to better the current world land speed record for this particular course.

Bracing myself in the far corner of the backseat, I hold on tight for what has become a terrifying real-life version of "Mr. Toad's Wild Ride." Feeling as though my bladder is going to burst, I wait for as long I can before blurting out that I really need to go to the bathroom. Muttering darkly to himself, Stu just keeps right on driving. Before I can ask the question again, he suddenly slams the car to a skidding stop in the middle of nowhere and points to the side of the road. After relieving myself as quickly as I can in the green and purple bracken and heather, I slide back into the car and off we go again.

///

That Stu did not particularly like me, I already knew. As I would later learn, none of it was personal. What with my American accent, long hair, beard, blue denim work shirt, and jeans, I simply reminded him of all those dreadful hippies who had persuaded the Stones they would encounter nothing but peace, love, and flowers when they took the stage during the free concert at the Altamont Speedway in northern California in December 1969.

With nothing to do to pass the time but talk as we headed toward Manchester, I started telling Jo Bergman about all the time I had spent backstage at the Apollo Theater in Harlem while doing my master's thesis on the storied music hall that even for the Stones had always been the high palace of American rhythm and blues. Naming just a few of the performers I had seen there week after week while standing in the wings, I talked about the great Joe Tex, Patti LaBelle, the Five Stairsteps, the Delfonics, and of course, "The Hardest Working Man in Show Business," "Mr. Dynamite," "Soul Brother No. 1," the inimitable James Brown.

Going into far too much detail, I then described the day when the disc jockey who had been scheduled to emcee the first show at the Apollo failed to appear and I suddenly found myself being shoved toward a backstage microphone on which a list of all the acts had been taped. In a voice I could barely recognize as my own as it boomed through the theater up to the balcony where only winos and glue-heads ever sat for the early show, I then proudly announced, "Ladies and gentlemen, welcome to the Apollo Theater."

As the legendary rock promoter Bill Graham once said about having won the Wednesday night amateur Latin dance contest at the Palladium Ballroom in New York City, "Why should I ever want to be President of the United States?" Much like him, I also felt like I had already done something better by getting to announce that show at the Apollo one afternoon.

What I did not know at the time was that just like me, both Mick and Keith had made their own obligatory white boy pilgrimage to the Apollo. Journeying up to Harlem on their first visit to New York in 1964, they had watched James Brown do his mad "Jump back, Jack / See you later, alligator," shimmy on one leg while exhorting the crowd to madness by falling in utter exhaustion to the stage and being led off into the wings wrapped in a purple cape, only to miraculously return once more dancing even harder than before.

The effect of Mick and Keith's visit to the Apollo can be plainly seen in Charlie Is My Darling, *the documentary of the Rolling Stones' tour of Ireland a year later. Perched on one leg as he performed on the bare stage of a movie theater with no theatrical lighting, Mick looked for all the world like a white and skinny version of none other than the great James Brown himself.*

The point of all this being that at a time in the music business when all credentials were entirely personal and what mattered most was whether or not you really loved the music, I had just introduced myself to Ian Stewart as someone whose life had also been irrevocably altered by the power of rhythm and blues.

///

Never once turning around to look at me, Stu just keeps right on driving with both hands on the wheel and his eyes firmly fixed on the road ahead. Long before he is ready to stop the car again, I say, "Stu, I don't know how to tell you this but I really have to go to the bathroom again." This time, his reaction is entirely different. Shaking his head as he begins to laugh, Stu says, "God, you're just like Brian, ain't you? He always had to stop as well whenever we were headed somewhere." And from that moment on, for reasons I did not then understand, I am okay with Stu.

When at long last we pull up in front of the Manchester Free Trade Hall, a gaudy Italian palazzo of a building built in the 1850s, a long-haired freak standing outside the front door is asking everyone who passes by for tickets. Brushing past him, I follow Jo Bergman inside the hall only to find that Keith Richards is already there. Shockingly on time for a change, he sits by himself in a garish, fluorescently lit dressing room, plunking away on a guitar.

With showtime drawing near, Mick sits in a chair staring at himself in a mirror as Bianca, still wearing her outrageous wide-brimmed hat, carefully makes up his eyes. Having finished applying mascara, she then goes to work on his cheeks with a wide brush.

Although the Stones are only twelve minutes late for the first show, a bit of slapstick that could have come right out of the English music hall takes place in the corridor outside their dressing room. Two ancient geezers who look as though they have worked in this building since the hall was built start talking about why Mick Jagger is not yet onstage.

Like he knows this for a fact, the first ancient geezer says, "E's 'avin' a quick jump with his girlfriend before the show."

"Naw," the other replies. "E's 'avin' his left ball tattooed."

"His left one? Why's that?"

Leaning in close, the first one says, "E's only got one, y'know."

Decked out in checkered cloth caps, ill-fitting jackets, and trousers that were now much too big for them held up by suspenders, or "braces" as they were called in England, old men just like them could be found backstage wherever the Stones went on this tour. Wizened relics from another age who would not have known one Rolling Stone from another if their lives depended on it, most of them were civil employees who had held their jobs for years and so were not about to do anything that might cost them their weekly pay packet.

Asked to perform even the simplest task before a show, their response was always, "Oh, I can't do that. It's more than me job's worth." Having somehow managed to survive two world wars as well as the terrible food rationing in England that had kept Ian Stewart from ever getting to eat a banana until he was seven years old, they were all members in good standing of the generation that had always considered the Stones an affront not just to national dignity but moral rectitude as well. Since it was utterly pointless to argue with them about doing anything for the Stones before they performed because it was always more than their job was worth, no one ever even tried.

Onstage before a packed house during the first show in Manchester, Mick Taylor takes two soaring blues solos in "Love in Vain." After the Stones do a twelve-minute version of "Midnight Rambler," Jagger attacks Chip Monck with an open bottle of champagne to wish him a happy thirty-second birthday onstage. As always, Mick then ends the show by flinging the basket of flower petals as he leaps into the air.

///

In the world of rock 'n' roll circa 1971, no one had a more impressive onstage résumé than Edward Beresford Monck, who had always been called "Chip" ever since he was a boy. Best known as the reassuring voice from the stage that had warned the crowd at Woodstock to stay away from the brown acid, Chip had been dosed by Owsley at Monterey Pop, helped Bill Graham renovate the Fillmore East, and lost five teeth after a Hells Angel smacked him in the mouth with the weighted end of a pool cue at Altamont.

A tall, lean, and rangy man with long reddish-brown hair, a huge mustache, and the regal bearing of a New England aristocrat, Chip had first seen the Stones perform at the Boston Garden in 1967. As he would later say, "They just stood there and played and so I tried to do something more decorative and creative with them."

After being hired by the band for their 1969 American tour, Chip put together the first lighting system ever to go out on the road with a rock 'n' roll band. To a great degree, what happened each night on this tour when the Stones performed "Midnight Rambler" was due to Chip. For when Mick Jagger slapped that studded belt against the stage and all the lights suddenly went blood red in his face, everyone in the house knew they were watching an authentic theater piece.

Before each show began, Chip would help set the mood for what was to come by playing songs like "Hard Headed Woman" by Cat Stevens. Once the show was over, Chip would send the audience home by playing a version of "Lady Jane" from which he had removed the vocal track, thereby making it into what he would later call "a beautiful piece of instrumentation. Like a madrigal, really. 'Have a good evening, get home safely, we look forward to seeing you the next time around.'"

An artist in his own right who would sometimes laughingly refer to Mick Jagger when he was not around as "His Ladyship," Chip always made it plain to his crew that being on the road with the Stones was not a party and they were not to associate with the band under any circumstances unless they were asked to do so—which of course never happened.

And although Chip would later say that by this point in his career he had "already gotten to the point where I realized production was three fingers under the elbow as the artist crossed the street and not something that was supposed to rival the music," his nightly contribution to what the Stones were then doing onstage was most definitely a significant part of the overall mise-en-scène.

//

Sitting together in a corner of the dressing room between shows, Charlie Watts turns to Bill Wyman and says, "Why aren't we staying in the Piccadilly Hotel here?"

"Banned," Bill tells him.

"What?" Charlie says. "Banned? Not us. Jagger's a film star now."

"Not him," Bill says. "Us. Last time we were here, Brian was throwing pillows out of a fourteenth-floor window. Blame it on the night porter then."

///

As he would soon demonstrate in no uncertain terms on this tour, Bill Wyman was already the walking history of the Rolling Stones. Unlike Mick and Keith, Bill forgot nothing and had only to consult the extensive journals he had so carefully kept over the years to know precisely what the band had been doing on any given day. A compulsive collector, Bill also saved virtually every last piece of Stones memorabilia that ever came through his hands.

When it came to putting up with Mick and Keith, Bill was in many ways just as long-suffering as Charlie, and there were endless tales of Bill walking into the studio only to discover that Keith had gone ahead and put his own bass line on a song without ever bothering to inform Bill about what he was doing.

A sexual privateer of the first order who also kept a complete log of all the women he slept with on the road, Bill was accompanied on this tour by the lithe and lovely Astrid Lundstrom, whom he had met in 1967 when she was an eighteen-year-old Swedish schoolgirl studying in London. Having been around the Stones long enough to be completely accepted by everyone, Astrid was then still so shy that she usually spoke only to Bill.

As she would later say, "Bands are male tribes and the Stones were always kind of making fun of Bill because he was too straight for them. In my opinion, he was incredibly straight. A bit rigid, a bit anal, and the sort of person who cataloged things. But quirky, no. I would have found that very appealing. I like quirkiness. But Bill was not quirky at all."

In Rolling with the Stones, *the massive, coffee table–sized book he co-authored with Richard Havers in 2002, Bill Wyman dutifully noted that shortly before the Stones began their farewell tour of Great Britain, he received a payment of $662 from former Stones' manager Allen Klein. Charlie Watts, Ian Stewart, and the estate of Brian Jones were all sent checks for $251, while Mick and Keith each received more than $805,000 in royalties, an enormous sum that would now be worth six to eight times that much. And so, despite the incredible amount of money the Rolling Stones owed the Inland Revenue in England, it was not as though either Mick or Keith was exactly broke at the time.*

According to Bill, precisely 34,400 people came to see the Stones perform on their farewell tour of Great Britain. Getting down to farthings and pence as only he could, Bill noted that the total gross receipts from the tour amounted to £25,800 (just a bit more than $60,000). After all the expenses had been deducted, the remaining sum was split so many ways among the Stones and their supporting cast of musicians that it seems clear even now that money was not the motivating factor for these shows.

In his book, Bill also included some of the articles about the Stones as well as reviews of their shows that appeared in various journals in England at the time, among them the Financial Times, *the* Yorkshire Post, *the* Record Mirror, *and the* Newcastle Journal. *Although the notices were almost uniformly favorable, referring to the Stones "as a piece of social history" and "still the best little* rock 'n' roll band in the world," *Bill himself was singled out for "his gravedigger's smile" and for looking onstage "as though he was waiting for a bus. But he didn't sound like it because he and the others played superbly."*

In the world according to Bill Wyman, that was just about all there really was to be said about the Rolling Stones' farewell tour of England.

///

As the time for the band to go out onstage to do the second show draws near, Mick suddenly gets to his feet and says, "I'm so zonked out. I need some energy." Like a boxer doing some fancy footwork before entering the ring for a championship fight, he starts running madly in place before leading the band out of the dressing room door.

Standing in what has now become my regular spot beside Chip Monck at the piano on the left side of the stage, I watch as the people sitting right down front reach out to the stage with their eyes closed and their hands held up before them like they are now praying that Mick Jagger will take them somewhere they cannot possibly go without him. Although none of this can hold a candle to the awful acid-induced madness that went down on the stage at Altamont, there is most definitely something truly frightening about it.

As we ride together to the hotel after the show in the backseat of a limo, Marshall Chess says, "You thought tonight was scary? You should have seen the show in Paris on the European tour last year. Real revolutionaries in that crowd, man. One guy wanted to pull me offstage because I was wearing a suit. Another guy came onstage and fell to his knees begging Mick to whip him. Three naked chicks came dancing out. It was crazy. In Germany, this Hells Angel had a gun. It only shot blanks, but we took it away from him. If he'd pulled it out during the concert, he would have been killed. Chip had these metal pipes onstage he used like javelins to keep the crowd away. Compared to that, tonight wasn't scary at all."

///

Having been declared persona non grata by all the establishments where they would have preferred to stay tonight in Manchester, the Stones instead found themselves stuck all the way out of town in a classic red brick British railway hotel located not all that far from a sign pointing appropriately enough to THE EDGE.

Out on the road with their girlfriends and small children in tow, the Stones no longer resembled the pop idols they had been back in 1966 in any way, shape, or form, and so the good news was that there was no way they would ever be banned from staying there again. The bad news was that they were all bored to death. With nowhere to go and nothing better to do, everyone congregated in a large room where no other guests were permitted to enter and proceeded to do all they could to entertain one another.

///

Speaking in a soft and halting voice, Gram Parsons, the brilliant singer-songwriter who left the Byrds to become a founding member of the Flying Burrito Brothers, and whom Marshall Chess now plans to sign to Rolling Stones Records, starts telling Charlie Watts about the night Bobby Keys walked into a studio to play on a session with Yoko Ono. "People were sniffing Excedrin and bouncing off the walls. And Yoko said, 'Bobby, imagine there is a cold wind blowing and you are a lonely frog.' Bobby Keys a frog. He just laid down his sax and played marimbas and tambourine and said, 'Lady, yew shore got a strange slant on things.' Yeah, starting with your eyes."

"Gram," Charlie says. "Fantastic."

Getting to her feet in the far corner of the room, a striking-looking young woman with a sharp-boned face, long red hair, glittering eyes, and pale, lightly freckled skin begins making her way toward the bar. Having given birth to Mick Taylor's daughter Chloe just two months ago, she seems far more direct and outgoing than the newest member of the Rolling Stones as well as very much at home in the company of rock stars.

///

Although I knew none of this at the time, Rose Millar (whom everyone always called Rose Taylor even though she and Mick Taylor were not yet married) was also on her first tour with the Rolling Stones. Described by her younger brother Robin, who in time would himself become a well-known record producer, as having "always been wild from the age of fifteen" as well as "car-stoppingly gorgeous," Rose had been expelled from the exclusive St. Paul's Girls' School in London. She had then gone to work in the editorial department of an advertising magazine while hanging out with rock stars like Peter Green of Fleetwood Mac, Georgie Fame, Long John Baldry, and Rod Stewart.

Giving up her job at Mick Taylor's request after they had begun living together, Rose had met the Stones for the first time while they were recording Sticky Fingers. *As she would later say, "I began going to the sessions at Olympic Studios and I couldn't believe how rude they all were. To each other, really. I was used* to bands who all got on well with one another but these people didn't have the same camaraderie and would turn up whenever they felt like it. Mick Taylor seemed to be there all the time as did Charlie and Bill but they were all absolutely always waiting for Mick or Keith."

While being out on the road with the Stones seemed, as Rose would later say, "a bit more exciting and better than the slog of the studio, the tour wasn't really fun because even at that point I think Mick Taylor realized he had made a mistake by joining them. Even then. Because he could have done other things. He could have gone and joined Paul Butterfield. He could have done music he was more interested in than rock 'n' roll. He could have played the blues. And jazz. He was also taking classical guitar lessons. His music interests were very wide and if he had done something that he had been the boss of, it would have been better for him than taking this job which of course everyone said, 'Oh, you have to do this. It's so wonderful.'

"In all the time he did it, he never ever thought it was wonderful. Ever. If he played well, it was okay except that Keith would turn his amp down. Or he would only have the time of his solo to play well and that was that. If he played badly, they applauded anyway so he felt there was no discernment on the part of the audience. He didn't feel he was making any contribution that was really important. He was so sensitive. And he was never satisfied with what he did with them, really."

Since Mick Taylor rarely said anything at all on this tour and seemed to be playing at the height of his powers on a nightly basis, no one had any idea how he was really feeling. Never shy about expressing herself, the same could not be said about Rose.

Catching sight of Keith as she nears the bar, Rose says, "Keith, I dreamed about you last night. You know that thing with the glass top you keep Marlon's toys in? You were standing with it on a sandy beach that was sinking and you said, 'Someone help me, or get me a drink.'"

As only he can, Keith says, "Get me a drink probably."

Carefully cutting slices from an apple which he then inserts one by one into a tall glass of Pimm's No. 1, a gin-based herbal liqueur no one else would ever think of drinking at this hour of the night, Keith adds, "I'll have to think about that one for a while." Taking his drink with him, he then quietly exits the room.

///

What no one knew back then was that shortly before the tour began both Keith and Gram Parsons had undergone a disastrous attempt at cleaning up by undergoing the apomorphine cure, recommended by Naked Lunch *author William Burroughs as the only way to stop using heroin. Lying side by side in a four-poster bed in Keith's house on Cheyne Walk, they had spent seventy-two hellish hours twitching from the treatment while throwing up into a bucket—only to then promptly begin using again once the treatment was done.*

Although Keith had not yet really interacted with anyone on the tour except for his companion, the blond and beauteous Anita Pallenberg, their young son Marlon, Gram Parsons, and his fellow musicians while they were onstage together, this too would change in time.

///

CHAPTER THREE

COVENTRY, MARCH 6, 1971

SATURDAY NIGHT IN COVENTRY, the small and picturesque city in the West Midlands where the Luftwaffe bombed St. Michael's Cathedral to ruins during World War II. Wearing a black-and-white-checked jacket, Mick Jagger sits quietly at a table in a restaurant between shows with his hands folded before him, drinking red wine. As some girl whom no one seems to know is hustled away through the front door, she cries out, "Forget my name, you bastard, you and all your Rolling Stones."

Taking a sip of wine, Mick says, "Boring, isn't it?"

Beside him, Bianca is talking about going gambling somewhere later this evening. Long after everyone else went to bed last night in Manchester, Mick, Marshall, and Bianca found themselves in a casino where they only let them lose and Mick dropped about £300, a sum Keith will later laughingly estimate as about half his total earnings from this tour.

"You even play gin rummy in a foreign language," Marshall tells Bianca. Since he already owes her about $8,000 in rummy debts, Marshall should know. "But that dealer in Manchester, he was terrible."

"Dealing out of a shoe, probably had three decks in there," Ian Stewart says. "Have to report him to the gaming commission, won't I?"

"Ah," Marshall says, "but if we had won, we'd all be saying how good he was, wouldn't we, Mick?"

After thinking about it for a moment, Mick says, "I don't care."

Around the phrase, a long moment of silence grows and grows. In many ways, it seems a lot like what happens each night when the Stones play "Wild Horses." The song is so powerful that it stops the audience dead in their tracks and for a long moment everyone just sits there thinking about it before they begin to applaud. Slowly, it dawns on everyone at the table that in terms of his gambling losses as well as so much else that is now going on around him on this tour, Mick simply does not care.

Picking up on this, Marshall says, "Oh, that was last night, huh?"

Leaning forward, Bianca asks Mick, "Tu vas changer le choix?"

If ever there was a time for Mick Jagger to consider altering the set the Stones have been doing onstage each night, this would be it. Performing before a young and strangely quiet audience during the first show, Mick did all he could to get the crowd on their feet but no matter how hard he tried, it did him no good at all.

The response was so muted that at the end of "Street Fighting Man" Mick did not even bother to throw the basket of flowers into the house. To ensure that everyone would get out of their seats at least once before leaving the hall, Chip Monck then played

"God Save the Queen," which did serve to keep the crowd on their feet until it was over.

With his mind already on something else, Mick looks at Bianca and says, "Choix de quoi?"

"De quoi, de quoi," she answers with a laugh.

Having had perhaps one drink too many tonight, one of the band's ladies wobbles a bit as she passes by the table. "Drunken bitch," Mick says. "She won't lose weight that way, will she?" Sighing just as he did before, he says, "Nothing to do but bitch, is there?"

Getting to his feet, Ian Stewart looks at Mick and says, "C'mon then. Intermission's over."

Showing some real emotion for the first time all night long, Mick says, "No. Don't wanna. Oh fucking why? They sold all the tickets here in three hours and then they just sat there."

To make him feel better, Stu says, "This was the most depressing part of the tour last time as well."

Walking over to the table, Charlie does a little soft-shoe routine that makes Mick smile and says, "Let's go out there and tread the boards then, Mick."

"Yeah," Mick says. "A tap dance. Oh, it's all right. But why do they just have to sit there? Let's go then. We'll do the same show. But if it's the same audience, we'll knock out a number and go home early, eh?"

In the dressing room as the Stones get ready to go back out onstage, the sound of Buddy Holly singing "Ready Teddy" comes spooling out of Bobby Keys's ever-present cassette recorder. As the next song starts Bobby says, "Mah golden saxophone is comin' up now." Born in Slaton, Texas, on the same day as Keith Richards,

Bobby is twenty-eight years old but still sometimes looks like the fresh-faced kid who first went out on the road with Buddy Knox and the Rhythm Orchids in 1961.

A spinner of tall tales who has definitely become the life of the party where the Stones are concerned, Bobby starts talking about how he played and recorded with Buddy Holly at K-Triple L radio in Lubbock and then appeared on the first Alan Freed show at the Brooklyn Paramount Theatre, which featured Buddy Holly and the Crickets, Clyde McPhatter, and the Everly Brothers backed up by Sam "The Man" Taylor's big band.

After carefully explaining to me how he learned to steam all the wrinkles out of his stage suit by hanging it in a hotel bathroom with a hot shower going full blast so he could then press his outfit to perfection beneath the mattress of his bed, Bobby says, "Ah been on the road sixteen goddamn years. That's why I am the way I am."

///

Because in every way possible he seemed to embody the wild outlaw spirit that was at the heart of rock 'n' roll, I just could not get enough of Bobby Keys on this tour. With a mouth and a heart as big as Texas, he was every rock writer's dream come true, an endless source of colorful stories about how he had once shot craps with Major Lance in a nightclub in Muncie, Indiana, and seen Billy "Fat Boy" Stewart pull a gun on someone during an argument after a show.

Because it was all such great stuff, I dutifully reported what Bobby Keys told me word for word in the article I wrote about the tour for Rolling Stone magazine only to learn many years later that on this tour Bobby was working just as hard at creating his own legend as he did each night playing saxophone onstage with the Stones. Taking it point by point, here is the actual truth.

Far too young to have ever actually played or recorded with Buddy Holly, Bobby Keys was eleven years old when he saw Holly perform on the back of a flatbed truck at the grand opening of a gas station in Lubbock. Since Alan Freed did his first show at the Brooklyn Paramount in 1955 when Bobby was just twelve years old and neither Buddy Holly and the Crickets, nor Clyde McPhatter, nor the Everly Brothers appeared on the bill, that story was also not true. Nor had Bobby already been on the road for sixteen years in 1971.

What does seem to be true is that while he was working with singer Bobby Vee at the Texas State Fair in San Antonio in July 1964, Bobby Keys did see the Rolling Stones perform before a decidedly indifferent crowd who could not have cared less about their music. When the Stones came back to do their second show that night, Bobby told Brian Jones that pop groups in America always changed their clothes before going onstage, thereby prompting the members of the band to exchange what they were wearing with one another.

As Jim Price would later tell me, he and Bobby Keys had both flown to London after completing Joe Cocker's Mad Dogs and Englishmen tour with drummer Jim Gordon, bassist Carl Radle, and keyboard player and vocalist Bobby Whitlock to join forces with Eric Clapton in a new band that came to be called Derek and the Dominos. After rehearsing for about a week at Abbey Road studios, they realized, in Price's words, "Hey, this is a guitar and keyboard band and they don't need any horns."

Both musicians were about to return to Los Angeles when Mick Jagger called and asked them to come play on the sessions for Sticky Fingers. *A trained musician who could also play piano, Price came up with all the horn arrangements in which Bobby played the sax solos. Both Keys and Price then accompanied the Stones on their 1970 European tour.*

While I am certainly not the only journalist ever to be taken in by a charming but unreliable source, Bobby Keys was so completely irresistible in so many ways that even now I cannot find it in my heart to hold any of this against him. Thanks to the energy he and Jim Price brought to the Stones' music each night onstage, the band seemed in many ways to be completely reborn.

Despite all the braggadocio, Bobby had in fact spent most of his adult life out on the road smoking pot, drinking to excess, and taking as much Benzedrine as he could while traveling from one small town to another with a variety of bands on a bus. Which was why Bobby Keys was the way he was.

———————————————————————————————

Shutting off his cassette recorder in the dressing room, Bobby Keys carefully pulls a velvet jacket on over his ruffled black stage shirt. Grabbing his horn, he charges out into the hallway like a runaway Brahma bull. Bumping right into Mick, he says, "You gotta teach me some French, man."

Laughing out loud, Mick says, "Sure, Bobby."

"Want me to write some songs too?" Bobby asks. "They won't sell as much as yours but. . . . "

Before he can complete the sentence, the Stones walk out on-stage. And just like in the movies, the second show is a bitch. With the lights all green and purple in their faces, Mick and the boys incite the crowd to a near-riot. As Charlie cooks like crazy,

Mick puts the microphone between his legs and bends over so far during "Midnight Rambler" that his forehead actually touches the painted white wooden stage. Out in the house, everyone sweats and dances and then goes home happy.

Or as Bobby Keys shouted as the Stones trooped back onstage in Newcastle for their encore, "Goddammit, rock 'n' roll is on the road again!" And beyond any shadow of a doubt, so it is.

Long after the tour was over, the single image that stayed with me from Coventry was seeing Bianca standing in an empty backstage hallway playing with a yo-yo on a string she had wrapped around the wrong finger of her hand. Wholly engrossed in what she was doing and looking much like a young girl dressed up in black and white for a big Saturday night on the town, Bianca seemed completely oblivious to everything that was going on around her.

Along with her incredible beauty and the obvious hold she had on Mick, it was this quality that had driven many of those traveling with the Stones to utter distraction. A completely self-created creature who never spoke about herself, Bianca was, as Winston Churchill once said of Russia, a riddle wrapped in a mystery inside an enigma.

Nor did any of the quotidian details of her life to this point in time help explain who she really was. That Bianca had once been Michael Caine's girlfriend and had been living with the famed French record executive and world-class playboy Eddie Barclay when she had first met Mick six months earlier at a Stones show in Paris revealed precious little about her character or precisely what agenda she was now pursuing with Mick.

Unlike Anita Pallenberg, who had been a full-fledged member of the Rolling Stones' inner circle ever since she had first become Brian Jones's girlfriend, Bianca was a rank outsider. Making the current situation even more difficult for all concerned, she never tried to hide her complete disdain for the always funky, drug-fueled world of rock 'n' roll.

Doing his best to make a joke of it, Ian Stewart had rearranged the letters of Bianca's first name and begun calling her "Binaca." While driving at breakneck speed from Newcastle to Manchester, Stu had let Jo Bergman know how he really felt about Bianca's influence on Mick by muttering darkly under his breath, "That bird, she's pushin' him."

And so she was but in precisely which direction no one could say for sure. Because Bianca had such a deep connection to Mick, and because the Rolling Stones could not exist without him, her silent presence on this tour represented a distinct threat to the well-being of one and all. And so everyone always kept a watchful eye on her when she and Mick were together while doing their best to conceal their concern about what their future might entail.

As Astrid Lundstrom would later say, "There was a big split between Mick and Keith on the tour because Bianca was there. Because of her mere presence, Mick became totally different. Before, he was much more approachable and more of an artist, but Bianca fed all that social narcissistic stuff of his."

What no one then knew was that Bianca was two months pregnant with Mick's child. Considering the way everybody but Mick seemed to feel about her, this was on more than one level clearly a blessing in disguise.

CHAPTER FOUR

GLASGOW, MARCH 8, 1971

WELCOME TO GLASGOW, a city so drab and gray and hard and mean that it makes Newcastle and Manchester seem like Paris by comparison. As everyone boards the bus that will take them from the airport to the hall, Mick Jagger decides for reasons known only to him to sit down right beside me. Looking very French indeed today, Mick is wearing a tightly ribbed sweater, a long brushed-suede maxi-coat with a sheepskin lining and collar, and a plaid woolen cap perched backward atop his long, flowing hair. In the corner of his left eye, there is a tiny spot of blood.

Catching sight of a gaggle of giggling teenage girls lined up outside the window to gawk at him, Mick laughs out loud and says he hasn't seen anything like this since 1962. And then he begins to talk. In a rambling rap that seems to go in all directions at once, Mick starts telling me about the mystical aspects of Stonehenge and Glastonbury and then about all the time he recently spent in Bali, "which is a total culture for the arts where a whole village will stay up all night for an opera or a ballet."

For reasons that totally escape me, Mick and I then launch

into what soon becomes a long and very involved conversation in fairly rapid-fire French. When I ask Mick how he learned to speak the language, he replies, "En l'école [*in school*], en France un peu [*in France a bit*], et avec ma jeune fille [*and with my girl*.]" Talking about Bianca as she herself never does, Mick tells me she has lived all over the world ever since she was fifteen years old and has spent time in France, Japan, Hawaii, and Canada.

In response to a question about music that I finally break down and ask him, Mick says, "Oh, who listens to Chuck Berry anymore? I mean, I haven't listened to that stuff for years. Rock 'n' roll has always been made by white suburban bourgeoisie like Elton John. For God's sake, I listen to the MC5. I don't like to see one thing end until I see another beginning. Like, for instance, breaking up with a woman. Do you know what I mean?"

While I was not about to say this to him then, my best answer to this question would have been, "Actually, I have no idea whatsoever." In his own inimitable way, was Mick trying to tell me that the chapter in the band's history that had begun on the fateful day in October 1961 when Keith Richards came over to talk to him on the train station in Dartford because of the albums Mick was carrying, Chuck Berry's One Dozen Berrys *foremost among them, was now over?*

Or was he referring to the manner in which he had finally decided to end his long-standing relationship with Marianne Faithfull after being told in no uncertain terms by Ahmet Ertegun, the legendary founder of Atlantic Records, that her increasing dependence on heroin was putting the future of the Rolling Stones in jeopardy?

Unwilling to be so gauche as to try to conduct an actual interview with Mick as we rode together on that bus, I was not about to ask. What I also did not know back then was that the stage was not the only place on which Mick performed. Because Mick was always on, his entire life was a performance and so there was never any knowing what was real and what he was doing purely for the effect it would have on the audience for whom he was performing, which in this case happened to be me.

What I can say for certain is that once Mick had given you his total attention, you found yourself willing to do almost anything to get it back again. At close range, his personality was just as addictive as any of the most powerful drugs known to man.

Getting to his feet as the bus finally comes to a stop, Mick says, "I'm going to have to sit you down sometime so we can have a long rap about Bali." And then just as quickly as he appeared by my side, Mick hops off the bus and makes his way into the hall through a backstage door.

Located at 126 Renfield Street in central Glasgow, Green's Playhouse first opened in 1927 and looks as though no one has bothered to clean it since then. Paint peels off all the walls in long curling strips, the air vents are covered with thick black soot, the entire backstage area is lit by bare bulbs, and the dressing rooms are so small that you literally cannot turn around without bumping into someone. When I ask a local stagehand why the second balcony has been closed tonight, he says, "To keep the rattles doon."

As a band that has been together for a week opens the show by playing two songs written by Mick Jagger and Keith Richards, Bill Wyman sits backstage passing the time by talking about the days when a show by the Rolling Stones was still an invitation for the disaffected youth of England to demonstrate their general displeasure with any and all forms of authority.

"In a place like Birkenhead," Bill says, "we'd go out and start 'I'm gonna tell you how it's gonna be. . . .' Three bars in and they'd all come sweepin' over the stage and we'd be finished for the night and back in the hotel with a thousand quid. Girls leapin' from a forty-foot balcony and arrows in the paper the next day showin' where one of them had jumped from."

Shaking his head in wonder at how different it has all become over the course of the past seven years, Bill says, "I remember only one audience back then that didn't like us from the start. All the factories here in Glasgow close at the same time during the summer. 'Scots week,' they call it. They all go to Blackpool, which is two hundred miles down the coast, and drink and we played there on the last Saturday night and they were evil. The stage was six feet high so all we could see was heads. There were about thirty of them sitting right down front spitting at us. Because of our long hair, I guess, and their birds fancyin' us.

"Keith was covered in it and finally he said, 'If you do that one more time . . . ,' and the guy did it and Keith kicked him in the head and they all went wild and came at us. We ran off the stage right into a police car. Stu came back to the hotel later with a little piece of wood hangin' off a wire and said, 'Here's what's left of your piano.' They destroyed the chandeliers, tore up all the seats, and smashed the amplifiers. Charlie's cymbals were just twisted pieces of metal.

"When we played Glasgow back then, they barred all the shop windows and had us come into the hall through a police corridor lined with Alsatian dogs. Not that it mattered. The fans still smashed up a train, crushed and burned all the chairs in the hall, and caused $30,000 worth of damage. You'll never see that again, I don't think."

//

Not surprisingly, considering the context, the conversation in the dressing room then turned to the cataclysmic day when the Rolling Stones had performed at Altamont. Going off on a bit of a petulant rant as what he called "some lovely cocaine Keith left behind" went around the dressing room, Mick began complaining about writers like Ralph Gleason, the august cofounder of Rolling Stone *magazine, and Al Aronowitz of the* New York Post *by saying, "Ralph Gleason wasn't even there, man. He's made more money than anyone from Altamont. He should at least say he wasn't there. Al Aronowitz? He wasn't there either, was he?"*

While at this late date there would seem to be no point whatsoever in rehashing the long and complicated sequence of events that led up to the free concert Bill Graham would later call "the Pearl Harbor of rock," no one who was then not alive can truly appreciate the media shit-storm that was loosed upon the Rolling Stones in America after the Hells Angels hired to act as security guards stabbed a gun-wielding young black man named Meredith Hunter to death right in front of the stage. Insofar as the straight press was concerned, Altamont marked the end of the Aquarian dream that had begun just six months earlier at Woodstock.

Aside from David Crosby saying that real dues would have had to be paid if a musician had been killed at Altamont, by far the most astonishing comment about what had happened that day also came from Bill Graham. Unable to contain his fury, he said of Mick Jagger, "He's now in his home country somewhere— what did he leave behind throughout the country? Every gig, he was late. Every fucking gig, he made the promoter and the people bleed. What right does this god have to descend on this country this way? But you know what the greatest tragedy is to me? That cunt is a great entertainer."

What no one in America back then understood was that based on their history as narrated by Bill Wyman in the dressing room in Glasgow, the Stones had long since become accustomed to major riots breaking out at their shows as all the kids outside the hall began flinging bricks, stones, bottles, and anything else they could get their hands on at cops on horseback. As far as the band was concerned, none of this had much to do with them at all. Because the Rolling Stones were only trying to play their music when all hell broke loose and utter chaos ensued, they never took any responsibility for what happened after they stepped onstage.

What few people also seem to have noticed at the time was that just eight days after Altamont, the Stones performed at the Saville Theatre in the West End of London and then did two more shows a week later at the Lyceum on the Strand. The point being that once the Rolling Stones were back in England, everything *that had happened at Altamont was already behind them because they were now in fact safe at home once more.*

Yet another salient point that was completely lost in the shuffle was that the Stones themselves had no real idea just how violent the Hells Angels in America truly were. When the band had employed the British version of the motorcycle gang to police their free concert in Hyde Park in July 1969 at which Mick memorialized the recently departed Brian Jones by reading a passage from Shelley in his honor, many of the British Hells Angels actually arrived by bus, thereby prompting members of the pop press to dub them "Hell's Herberts," the name "Herbert" being an English slang term for a hapless loser.

That the hippie dream had clearly ended long before the Rolling Stones ever took the stage at Altamont would have been apparent even back then to anyone who had lived in the Haight-Ashbury before LSD was made illegal in California in 1966. However, it was no accident that the Rolling Stones brought this point home to both the mainstream and counterculture media in America. For as Kris Kristofferson then sang, it was always easier to blame it on the Stones.

Released just three months before the English tour began, Gimme Shelter, *the astonishing documentary film about Altamont by Albert and David Maysles, had served not only to start the conversation all over again but also to make many of those who saw it wonder if there was in fact any hope left for a generation that had once defined itself in terms of peace, love, and flowers. And while both Mick Jagger and Charlie Watts had allowed themselves to be filmed in the documentary viewing what had happened at Altamont, none of it seemed to have affected the Rolling Stones themselves in any substantive way.*

Along with so much else the Stones had seen and done, Altamont was now firmly in their past. And so it should come as no surprise that no one on the tour ever talked about it again.

///

Getting to their feet, the band walks out the dressing room door. As Mick makes his way through the hot, seedy, cramped basement corridor toward the stage in Green's Playhouse in Glasgow, he actually brushes shoulders with Rab Munro, the twenty-three-year-old lead singer of the band that just opened the show. Without breaking stride or exchanging a single word, they both continue heading in the completely opposite directions they will follow for the rest of their lives.

As soon as the Stones hit the stage, the 3,100 people who have packed this place to the rafters tonight go wild. As though they have been caught in some kind of weird time warp, all the brassy blond middle-aged women in pants suits who are sitting right down front leap from their seats and begin screaming like teenage girls while clutching their heads in ecstasy whenever Mick shows them his ass. Taking full advantage of the situation, Mick says, "I guess you want me to get on my knees and beg. I bet you want me to crawl. I bet you want me to howl."

And because yes indeed this is just what they want him to do, Mick promptly begins crawling across the front of the stage, driving them all even crazier than before. As Charlie pounds away at his bass drum and Keith rips one driving riff after another from his guitar, the women scream and shout and moan and cry in what may well be the first mass public female orgasm in Scottish history.

Backstage between shows, Bobby Keys puts on quite a performance of his own. Fixating on a girl who does some sort of clerical work for the theater, he decides to hit on her by saying, "Do you like rock 'n' roll? Do you watch TV? Do you like *The Man from U.N.C.L.E.?* Well, that's Illya Kuryakin right over there. Turn around, Charlie, he's a little shy. Goddammit, Charlie, turn around!"

After doing so, Charlie disappears just as quickly as he can into the dressing room. Turning back to the girl, Bobby Keys says, "What's your name, love?"

"Frances," she says.

"Frances," Bobby says, "do you like to get nekkid? Ah do. All nekkid and hot and sweaty? Let's you and me get all nekkid and jump into the pool. Have you ever made love with a saxophone player, Frances? Would you like to live in the country? Ah'll give up this life for you, Frances, ah swear. Just come home with me tonight."

As though keeping his band in check on the road is also part of his job, Mick puts an end to the conversation before the terrified girl runs screaming down the hall by saying, "Bobby? Come on now, Bobby. Time for us to go back onstage, eh?"

After doing a second show every bit as good as the first, the Stones and all those traveling with them begin settling into their seats on the midnight flight from Glasgow to London. Sitting next to Bobby Keys all the way at the back of the plane, Marshall Chess keeps saying, "Boogie, Bobby, boogie," as the two of them talk about old-time rock 'n' roll sax rides.

Across the aisle from them, Anita Pallenberg picks up on the phrase and begins crooning, "Boo-gey, boo-gey." Because of her accent, the word sounds like an errant German nickname for Humphrey Bogart.

By her side, Boogie, a small brown-and-white King Charles Spaniel puppy, is about to fall asleep in Keith Richards's arms. With the doors of the plane about to close, contentment positively flows from seat to seat as conversations buzz and hum. The seat-belt sign is on and the engines are about to rev when a blue-jacketed airline official suddenly comes through the door.

Walking all the way back to where Keith and his dog recline, the official says, "That dog flies by prior arrangement only, sir. You'll have to get off the plane."

"What?" Keith says.

"I'm sorry, sir," the official tells him. "But I warned you in the airport. I don't know how you managed to slip by me onto this plane but you'll have to get off now."

"Look," Keith says, "I've flown BEA, TWA, Pan Am . . . to San Francisco, to places you and this airline have never been. . . ."

"You have to supply a box, sir," the official tells him.

"I happen to know that section of the Geneva Convention very well," Keith tells him. "You have to supply the box."

Can it be that Keith Richards has actually committed this particular section of the Geneva Convention to memory? Even if he has, that is not the point. Simply, no one tells Keith Richards what to do. As this poor beleaguered airline official is about to learn, no one ever has and no one ever will.

Taking the conversation to a whole other level, Keith says, "This is ridiculous. It's an emergency. My wife and child are here and we have to get home so we can take our child to a doctor tomorrow."

Although Keith and Anita are in fact not married and Marlon himself seems to be the very picture of good health at the moment, the real truth is always what Keith Richards needs it to be at any given moment in time. Not realizing just how far in over his head he has gotten himself here, the official says, "I'm sorry, sir."

"We just want to get home," Keith says. "Is it that important? Just let us leave."

Firmly standing his ground, the official says, "The rules, sir."

"I know the rules," Keith tells him. "Get this plane going. We're not moving."

Spinning on his heel, the official walks back down the aisle and leaves the plane only to return with two large Scottish policemen in blue uniforms in tow. "What's the law doin' here?" Mick calls out loudly. "Come to arrest us all, have you? Oy! You, you, oy!"

Naked to the waist save for the blue nylon windbreaker Ian Stewart gave him after he threw his sweat-soaked T-shirt into the house at the end of the second show, Mick Jagger is lying flat on his backbone in a seat on the aisle. Turning his head the other way, the big Scottish cop now towering over Mick does his best to ignore him.

"Oy, *oy!*" Mick says again. And then, just like the saucy English schoolboy he so often seems to be, Mick reaches out to jangle the cop's sleeve with his hand.

Leaning over Mick, the cop says, "Now, now, chummy, no one's done nothin' yet. Why should we arrest anyone?"

"He's come to arrest the dog," Keith says.

"What are you doing here?" Mick demands. "A little dog like that. A puppy. You should be ashamed." As his face collapses in a look of utter dismay, Mick wails, "Who called the law? Arrest us."

"Chummy," the cop says.

"Chummy?" Mick demands.

"Sir, look," the cop says.

Quickly shifting gears, Mick says, "Don't curse me. I saw you say 'fuck.' Don't go cursing me."

Beautiful, Mick. All the cops have to do now is search the luggage and find the little brown medicine jar of cocaine with a pound note wrapped around it for convenient use that was going around the dressing room tonight and everyone will immediately be escorted to a Glasgow jail.

Taking command of the situation just as he did when Bobby Keys was out of control backstage between shows, Mick says, "Anita, go find the captain."

Beautiful, Mick. What better way to solve this problem than by sending Mata Hari Anita, who tonight is a vision in crocheted stockings, highly-polished black leather boots, and a pair of hot pants that leave nothing to the imagination, into the cockpit to seduce the captain of this plane as it stands on a runway in Glasgow?

"Gooo," Mick suddenly says. Across the aisle, Marlon laughs happily as he repeats the word right back at Mick. Surrounded on all sides by little kids, slinky ladies, and crazy rock stars, the bewildered cops realize they are outflanked on every level.

Trying to come up with a solution that will make everyone happy, Marshall Chess says, "We'll put the dog in Charlie Watts's orange bag. Is that okay?"

"Yes," says one of the cops.

"No," says the airline official.

"You brought him on the plane and now the two of you can't agree," Keith shouts.

"How about mah rattlesnake?" Bobby Keys yells. "Can ah keep him up here?"

"How about my vulture?" Jim Price asks.

With words whizzing back and forth across the aisle like bricks in a street fight, Keith says, "Ya Scots git. Get off the plane!"

"Arrest us," Mick demands again.

With the flight now already fifteen minutes late, a hurried conference is convened at the front of the plane so the stewardesses, the pilots, the cops, and the airline official who started all this in the first place can discuss the situation among themselves.

"We'll link arms," someone calls out.

"Arrest us," Mick demands yet again.

Walking up the aisle with the only piece of luggage Charlie Watts brought with him tonight, Marshall Chess grants one of the cops a battlefield promotion and says, "Look, Lieutenant, how's this bag here?"

Finally conceding, the airline official says, "If you put the dog in the orange bag, he can ride in the hold."

"What's your name?" Keith demands.

"Never you mind," the official says. "It's not important."

"Ah, but it is," Keith tells him. "If this dog dies, I'll see that it does become important. If he freezes to death in the hold. . . ."

Trundling Boogie off the plane in Charlie's orange bag, the airline official puts him in the hold and at long last the plane finally takes off. When it screeches to a halt an hour and a half later on the runway in London, there is a moment of sheer terror as yet another bottle containing half an ounce of cocaine with a current street value of $500 in England somehow hits the floor before being quickly grabbed and put safely away again for later use.

As for Boogie, he doesn't freeze to death at all but instead comes spilling and sliding across the polished airport floor with his tail wagging happily as Keith gathers him into his arms. Climbing into a brace of waiting chauffeur-driven Bentleys and long black Dorchester limousines, everyone speeds home and the incident is quickly forgotten by one and all. Call it just another minor laugh-filled moment on tour with the Rolling Stones.

CHAPTER FIVE

BRISTOL, MARCH 9, 1971

THE KIDS IN BRISTOL MAY BE SHARP as a pistol but the seven ushers standing in front of the stage are thick, bearded wrestlers in silk suits who stop anyone from dancing if they even dare to get out of their seats. During "Street Fighting Man," Mick places a small mound of flowers atop each of the ushers' heads like an offering. As if by magic, all the kids start dancing and the Stones then go out to do an encore. Going even further during the second show of the night, Mick kicks one of the ushers in the shoulder as he drags a pretty young girl off the stage.

Aside from Keith looking for Ian Stewart in the dressing room before the first show because "he has some very important pills I can't go onstage without" and then asking, "Where are joints? I can't find any in my bags," nothing much happens in Bristol. And so for the Stones and all who travel with them, it becomes just another stop along the road.

What I do find of great interest now was that earlier in the day both Mick and Charlie were making their way down the platform in London's Paddington Station when the conductor announced that the train to Bristol was about to leave. Running for it, Charlie slipped through the doors of the nearest car just in time. Because Mick could not be bothered to do the same, the train pulled out two steps ahead of him and he had to catch a later one to make it to the gig in time.

Aside from demonstrating the fundamental differences in their personalities, this was Mick acting like a rock star on the road as opposed to the wealthy and successful businessman he would have no doubt become if he had seen fit to complete his studies at the London School of Economics rather than pursue a career singing with a rock 'n' roll band.

As Tony Smith, who was promoting this tour with his father John, would later say, "As always, Mick was the one who was basically the manager. And I do remember that when the tickets went on sale before the tour started, I was sitting at home on a Saturday afternoon when the phone went and it was Mick saying, 'I just heard that in Bristol people are being allowed to buy more than two tickets each.' We had limited the amount of tickets you could buy because they were so much in demand and Mick was on the case and checking all the box offices to make sure it was being dealt with properly and here he was on the phone with me. So he was very much on the ball."

And there you have it in a nutshell. The English schoolboy persona that always served Mick so well when he pulled it out of his grab bag of personalities on this tour was just one of the many roles he was so adept at playing. Unlike Keith, Mick Jagger was a shape-shifter of major proportions. As Keith would later say of Mick, it was like dealing "with a nice bunch of guys."

And now a word about Charlie Watts. Unfailingly polite and always hysterically funny in his own unique deadpan manner, it had become apparent even to me by this point in the tour that in actual fact Charlie was the one around whom all the other Stones revolved. Without him, they would still have been the Rolling Stones but the fun factor would have most certainly been diminished a thousandfold.

Unlike Mick and Keith and the late Brian Jones, Charlie had never taken acid and so his soul had not been psychedelicized. While he might have a quick smoke before walking out onstage or drop the occasional upper to keep himself going on the road, Charlie was still the same person he had always been. As hip as they came and sharp as a razor, Charlie Watts was a living, breathing throwback to a time when jazz musicians were content to be just that and nothing more because the concept of rock stardom had yet to be introduced to the world.

Although Charlie was the steady throbbing heart of the band onstage, the Stones themselves did not follow him when they played. Because Charlie followed Keith and was always a bit behind while Bill Wyman tended to be in front, thereby causing the overall rhythm to wobble at times, it was not unusual to see Keith charge over to the drum kit like a madman in the middle of a song while screaming at Charlie to pick up the beat. If this bothered him in any way whatsoever, he never let it show.

Aside from his musicianship, it was also Charlie's endless ability to put up with all the madness that came with being a Rolling Stone that enabled him to remain at the center of their very small and completely incestuous world. If you asked Charlie a question back then, he would always give you a straight answer. Although he looked like Buster Keaton and still dressed like the graphic designer he had become after attending Harrow Art School, there was something so artless and charming about Charlie's personality that everyone on the tour always wanted to be around him.

Far more than any of the other Stones, Charlie was grounded. And so if anyone had told me he would go through some serious personal changes later in his life and then actually punch Mick Jagger in the face after becoming outraged by what Mick said to him over the phone at five in the morning in a hotel in Amsterdam in 1983, I would have called that person a liar. What I can say for certain even now is that back then Charlie was not just a sweetheart of major proportions but also most definitely everyone's darling.

CHAPTER SIX
BRIGHTON, MARCH 10, 1971

AS I SIT BY HIS SIDE IN THE BACKSEAT of the long black limo that has just picked me up outside my flat in London for the ninety-minute drive to Brighton, Marshall Chess reaches into his jacket pocket for a joint of what he says is the finest Jamaican weed. Firing it up, he takes a hit and then offers it to me.

"Marshall," I say. "I can't."

"C'mon, man," he says. "This is great stuff. And it's my last joint."

"You said that last night," I tell him.

"So what?" he says. "This is the last one, I swear. Go on. Take a hit."

Knowing he will pull this exact same routine on me the next time I see him, I do as I have been told. On this tour, Marshall Chess is a constant source of not just fine Jamaican weed but also the kind of boundless energy and enthusiasm that made him the perfect choice to run the Stones' brand-new record label. Having just split up with his wife, Marshall is now so fully involved in being what he will later call "the creative director" of the Rolling

Stones that there is nothing he will not do to help the band. What I like best about him is that all we ever seem to do together is laugh at everything on a nonstop basis.

///

Needless to say, getting high back then was something quite different than the quasi-legal, rather ordinary lifestyle it has since become. Being in an altered state during this era was not a means of coping with what then passed for reality. Rather, it was a victory over the boring stupidity of the straight world, a declaration of individual independence, and also the easiest way to pretend you were someone you were not.

Within the protective web that surrounded the Stones, you could get as high as you liked without ever worrying about where you had left your bag or how in the world you were going to get back to the hotel at four in the morning in a city where all the public transport had long since shut down for the night. Being high around the Stones only reinforced the feeling of youthful invincibility that was then the essence of rock 'n' roll. So long as you were with the band, nothing bad could ever happen to you. Or so it seemed to me back then.

///

In Brighton, the seaside resort where day-trippers from London have traveled by train to enjoy themselves by the sea for the past 130 years, the Stones are scheduled to play two shows in a 1920s dance hall that has been converted into an oversold, very smoky, and completely hellish ballroom called The Big Apple.

For the first and only time on this tour, due to what no doubt must have been some kind of mistake on their part, Keith, Anita,

Marlon, and Gram Parsons actually arrive at the gig on time only to find that the dressing room door is locked. Making matters just that much worse, no one seems to know where to find the key. Taking immediate charge of the situation, Marshall Chess sends off a variety of envoys to locate the hapless local promoter.

Trapped in a dark, dank corridor as deadly cold as only a corridor in England could then be, the Stones and all who travel with them wait for someone to come unlock the door. As they stand there shifting impatiently from foot to foot with their breath forming steaming clouds in the freezing air, the minutes seem to pass like hours. That the Rolling Stones cannot even get into their own dressing room before the show is an outrage that Keith Richards soon chooses to take completely personally.

As he has already proven on this tour, Keith is not just a consummate musician onstage but also a world-class performance artist who at a moment's notice is perfectly willing to transform any situation that does not meet his needs into high drama. Cradling baby Marlon in his arms, Keith says, "The bloody nerve. Making us wait out here. Who do these people think they are?"

That no one can answer this question only seems to make Keith even angrier. What has been just another minor moment of annoyance on the road suddenly becomes something else again when Marlon starts to cough. Although the child still seems to be as healthy as a horse, the wheels in Keith's brain begin spinning even faster than before.

In his mind, poor Marlon has now suddenly become a waif, a poor and pitiful orphan of the storm whom much like Tiny Tim will be lucky to get a hard crust of bread to eat on Christmas Eve. Exposed to these conditions, poor little Marlon's cough could suddenly become the croup. And then simply because some promoter has forgotten where he put the key to the dressing room door, Keith's beloved baby boy could expire right in his arms. Not that this is going to happen. But it *could*. And so when Marshall tells Keith that everyone is still waiting for the promoter to appear, Keith says, "Sod the bloody promoter. The filthy lout. Who do these people think they are?"

Working the scene for all he is worth, Keith stomps angrily back and forth across the narrow corridor a few times while continuing his diatribe. Finally deciding to take action, he hands Marlon to Anita and launches a full frontal assault on the door. *Rattle-rattle* goes the knob in his hand. *Bam-bam-bam* goes the flat of his palm against the frame.

Realizing this door is not just most definitely locked but also so sturdy that it is not about to give way, Keith reaches into his pocket for the single tool he is never without. Producing a knife, he promptly starts going to work with the tip of the blade on the screws that hold the hinges of the door in place. Although I have yet to exchange a single word with Keith on this tour and doubt he even knows who I am or what I am doing here, I have now become such an integral part of the Stones' traveling party in my own mind that before I know it I am standing right beside Keith with a metal comb in my hand doing all I can to help him.

Twist-twist-twist, out come the screws one after another. Like a pair of safecrackers working on a vault in the Bank of England, neither one of us speaks as we focus on the task at hand. Sagging backward, the door suddenly falls open before us. Hauling it into the dressing room, we fling it to the floor and then stand back so everyone can file past us into what for the Stones before a show is always a safe haven where no one but those they know and trust can ever go.

When at long last the promoter finally shows up with a set of keys dangling from his hand, everyone just ignores him. Innocent as newborn babes, none of them has any idea at all who could have done this dastardly deed. Having just aided and abetted Keith Richards in committing the crime of breaking and entering in the name of justice, rock 'n' roll style, I now feel certain that I do in fact belong on this tour.

//

Dear old Keith. What a lad indeed he was back then. Unlike Mick, Keith seemed to have no interest whatsoever in high society, nor any real need to seek approval from anyone but what was often overlooked about him was the aspirational aspect of his personality. As working-class as he had been raised and still so often seemed to be in many ways, Keith always gravitated to the company of natural-born aristocrats who, just like him, had been born with the gift of laughter and a sense that the world was mad.

Unwilling to cut his conscience to fit this year's fashions, Keith never met his betters on any terms but his own. What you saw with Keith was what you got. If you liked it, great. You could join the party and try to hang out with him for as long as your system would allow. If not, then you could just ride on, baby, and find something else to do with your precious time.

Much like Mick, Keith could also sometimes be truly impossible to control. Shortly before the tour began, Keith had set everyone's nerves on edge by failing to show up at all in the studio for the session during which the Stones had cut "Moonlight Mile," the final track on Sticky Fingers. *Asked if this had caused any tension between Mick and Keith, a longtime Stones insider who was on the tour would later say, "Well, if your lead guitarist doesn't turn up for the session when you're cutting the final track on your new album, I'm sure there's bound to be a bit of tension, yes. Whether Mick accepted it is another question because he'd already seen what had happened to Brian and might have thought, 'Here's another casualty waiting to happen.'"*

While this was in fact precisely the kind of behavior Brian Jones had exhibited before being asked to leave the band, Keith was made of far sterner stuff. Despite how out of it he had seemed at times during the 1970 European tour, Keith had still somehow made it through all those gigs intact. The man's commitment to the Rolling Stones was so deep that even if he was at death's door, everyone knew Keith would always be there when the show began.

Already well on his way to developing the full-blown Pirate King persona he would refine over the coming years into a character only Johnny Depp could have played on screen, Keith had not yet ever spoken to anyone at length for publication. He was the one who made the music while Mick did all the talking. Long before they ever became known as "The Glimmer Twins," this was an arrangement that seemed to suit them both perfectly.

It was not until I spoke to Keith again recently for a book on which I was then working that I realized how much this aspect of his personality had changed over the years. After so many phone calls notifying me precisely when he would come on the line that I began wondering if I was about to speak to the President of the United States, I picked up the phone in my office only to hear Keith shout out my name as though it had been only a few days since we had last seen one another.

Although the topic at hand was supposed to be the life and times of Ahmet Ertegun, Keith began telling me that the reason

Phil Spector had been so good at recording in mono was because he was deaf in one ear. Although Phil could also sometimes be an asshole, Keith said he was now thinking of sending him a cake in jail. When I asked if the cake would contain a file, Keith said, "No, a bomb!"

Unable to help myself after yet another particularly outrageous comment, I said, "Keith, you are so fucking politically incorrect." Laughing out loud, Keith replied, "Yes, and it's all quotable, man!" True that, both then and now.

///

Before the first show begins, a writer and a photographer from some German magazine wander into the dressing room. Clad in shiny black leather, they both look as though Erich von Stroheim has chosen them from central casting to play these parts. When someone asks them what they are doing here, the writer says he is looking for "Mick Jagga, ja?" Led off to the far corner where Mick sits, the writer starts firing questions at him as the photographer snaps madly away.

Getting ever weirder, the night wears on. At some point, someone asks me to take Gram Parsons upstairs so he can watch the show. Gram is so loaded tonight that he can barely see. His eyes are slits in his face, he is slurring his words, and his skin is so deathly pale that I am afraid to ask how he is feeling. That there is no way he will ever find the stage on his own is obvious.

Eager to be of service, I lead Gram out into the still-freezing corridor. Pushing open the door I think will lead us into the cavernous hall where 2,000 sweaty kids are smoking as much hash as they can to prepare themselves for the Stones, we instead find ourselves standing before a steep flight of stairs. Since the only way to go is up, I lead Gram to a landing only to discover that the door is locked.

Up two more flights of stairs we go, only to encounter yet another locked door. With no other choice, we keep on climbing. Feeling like a kid trapped changing classes in a high school of the perpetually damned, I look over my shoulder to see how Gram is doing. With his breath so labored that he cannot speak and his face even more deathly pale than it was before, Gram Parsons is now seriously losing it in every possible way.

Knowing this is not cool at all and I am failing miserably at taking care of Gram in the manner to which he has long since become accustomed, I start climbing the stairs faster than before. After what seems like an eternity even to me, I finally find a door that has not been locked. When Gram joins me, I shove open the door and we walk through it together only to find ourselves standing on the completely deserted balcony of a huge movie theater.

Right in front of us on a screen that looks to be at least twenty feet high and twice as wide, the extremely awful movie *Myra Breckinridge* is being shown in very lurid living color. As Raquel Welch, Mae West, and John Houston cavort before us like overblown figures from a fever dream by Hieronymus Bosch, Gram and I look at one another in horror. Both of us know we have entered another dimension. Gram Parsons and I are now in the twilight zone.

Getting out of there just as fast as we can, Gram and I run back down the stairs like the hellhounds are on our trail. Making our way back to the dressing room, we head to the other end of the corridor, go up some stairs, and walk through an open door into what looks like a big barn of a discotheque. Because the wooden floor beneath us is sprung, it actually moves up and down when we step on it, thereby making everything seem even more surreal.

After I finally deposit Gram Parsons by the side of the stage, I start apologizing for having led him on a nightmare journey I am fervently hoping he is much too stoned to remember for long. While I would like to say I am doing this out of concern for him, the truth is that I am far more worried about how all this might affect my standing with the Stones. When I am done telling Gram how truly sorry I am, he just looks at me. Opening his mouth to speak for the first time since we left the dressing room, he says, "Wow, man. *Wow.*" And then, just like the ghost he will soon become, Gram Parsons turns his back and vanishes into the crowd.

Although it is still freezing cold in the downstairs corridor outside the dressing room, it is so hot inside the Big Apple itself that when the Stones finally take the stage for the first show of the night no one can stay in tune for long. No doubt to express their enthusiasm for what they are hearing, kids in the audience begin heaving the pillows on which they have been sitting toward the stage.

Spinning end over end in beams of red, green, and yellow light, the pillows come thudding down on the gear. When one of them knocks over the long brown tapered bottle of German white wine Bill Wyman always keep on top of his amp during the show, the Stones just go right on playing.

///

Having spent much of my free time on the tour writing lovesick poems about how lonely I was on the road, I ended up spending the night in Brighton with a lovely English girl named Julia who wore high lace-up boots and had an infectious smile. As I would later learn, she was the daughter of a full colonel in a British cavalry regiment. That he would not have hesitated to shoot me dead on sight from horseback for what she and I did together that night, I had no doubt. And although this turned out to be not just a one-night stand but the beginning of a brief but somewhat meaningful relationship that I still look back on fondly, I cannot now remember her last name for the life of me.

Riding back to London on the train the next day all by myself, I was high as a kite on the power that came from touring with the Stones. Although there was no black limo waiting outside Victoria Station to take me home, I realized that being on tour with the Rolling Stones was in fact the ultimate adolescent fantasy.

Getting to stay up just as late as you liked each night, you could order whatever you liked in any restaurant without ever having to pay for it and there was no one around to tell you what to do. The rush that came from being on the road with the band was so addictive that those who had already become far more accustomed to this lifestyle than me were always perfectly willing to do whatever was required in order to remain within the inner circle. No doubt about it. After just six days on the road with the Stones, I was hooked.

///

CHAPTER SEVEN

LIVERPOOL, MARCH 12, 1971

IN LIVERPOOL'S LIME STREET STATION, Mick steps off the train from Euston in London looking somewhat like an altar boy with his hair cut short. Although the storied Empire Theatre, where local luminaries like the Beatles, the Dave Clark Five, Gerry and the Pacemakers, the Searchers, and a host of others have all performed, is just half a block away and Mick could easily walk there in no time, it is still much too early for him to show up at the hall. With Bianca by his side, Mick slides instead into the backseat of a long black limo that takes them to the old, dark, cavernous hotel where they spend the rest of the afternoon. .

While Mick may in fact have nasty habits and take tea at three, the hotel is so boring that a few hours later he finds himself escorting Bianca into the tearoom off the lobby at the far more proper time of four o'clock. Sitting down at a table in the corner, they both watch the ancient waitress who looks like she has been working here forever shuffle slowly toward them while pushing a trolley stacked high with cups and saucers, pots of tea, and toast and jam.

Catching sight of Mick for the first time as she begins sliding a cup and saucer onto his table, the waitress suddenly straightens up and exclaims, "*You!* The last time you were here, you didn't pay the bill!"

Laughing out loud, Mick explains to Bianca that when the Stones played in Liverpool in 1966, a group of hysterical teenage female fans broke into the tearoom while he was there. Forced to flee for his life, Mick did in fact leave the bill behind. Promising the waitress he will not be doing this again today, Mick promptly charms her into serving him and Bianca tea.

Several floors above them in Marshall Chess's suite, things are not nearly so calm and civilized and for a very good reason. At the moment, no one knows where Keith Richards happens to be. Whatever rough jungle telegraph has kept Marshall and Jo Bergman apprised of Keith's whereabouts as he journeyed to every previous gig to which he was also late seems to have finally collapsed under its own weight today. With just two hours to go before the first show starts, Keith is, for want of a better term, missing in action.

Although Ian Stewart has already told me about the night the Stones went onstage in Aylesbury without Brian Jones after he had driven the wrong way in the fog and that the band did four shows without him during their 1964 American tour, this is a kettle of completely different fish. As a band, the Rolling Stones cannot even walk out onstage without Keith. In other words—no Keith, no show.

And so it is that as the afternoon wends on and the time to leave for the hall draws near, the general mood among those gathered in Marshall's suite gets just as dark as the oncoming night. Having spent a fair amount of his adult life waiting for Mick or

Keith to show up, Charlie Watts seems completely unconcerned about it all as he sits in an overstuffed chair in the living room avidly watching the latest episode of *Dr. Who*.

By this time, the popular BBC science fiction series has been on the air for so long in England that when I ask Charlie if he can help me understand it, he just throws his hands up in the air and says, "No, I can't. If you haven't seen the show since the start, it's impossible." Without another word, he then leans forward and directs all his attention to the screen.

Having sat as a teenager with my parents in my living room in Brooklyn each Sunday night watching one group after another from Liverpool perform on The Ed Sullivan Show *during the British Invasion in 1964, you might think that I would have been eager to leave the hotel to get my own look at this tough-as-nails, working-class city on the River Mersey from which all that great music had come.*

Stuck in limbo in a hotel that could have easily passed for the setting of a rock 'n' roll version of No Exit, the thought never even entered my mind. Being on the road with the Stones was so all-consuming that the central drama of the day—would Keith Richards make it to the gig?—was all that really mattered to me.

What I did come to realize as that seemingly endless afternoon wore on was just how much time the Stones spent waiting to go onstage while they were on the road. At times it must have seemed even to them that the waiting was all there really was. Which back then was about as existential as I ever got.

Backstage at the Empire Theatre, twenty people doing their best to pretend they have no idea what time it is crowd a very small dressing room waiting for Keith to arrive. With the first show already an hour late and Tony McPhee and the Groundhogs having long since finished their opening set, Chip Monck is now playing an extended version of his greatest hits collection to keep the crowd from freaking out.

Looking for all the world as though he was brought here by the same swirling black funnel cloud that transported Dorothy and Toto from Kansas to Oz, Keith Richards suddenly bursts through the dressing room door with Boogie in his arms. Although Keith's hair looks a bit ruffled, his face is completely unmarked and he does not seem to be bleeding from any of his extremities which means he should be able to go onstage tonight.

Having made what even on the Broadway stage would have to rank as one hell of a dramatic entrance, Keith does not bother to offer a single word of explanation as to why it has taken him this long to get here. Looking around the dressing room, he says instead, "Is there anything to smoke?"

Slouched on a couch next to Bianca in the far corner, Mick answers the question by quietly saying, "We have to go on. They've been waiting."

What makes Mick's statement truly remarkable is the complete lack of emotion in his voice. Having been through all this before with Brian Jones, Mick is not about to offer any kind of judgment whatsoever about Keith's behavior or let him know just how overwrought some people have been all afternoon long. In situations like this, that is simply not what Mick Jagger does. And while everyone including Mick would love to know where the hell

Keith Richards has been all day long, this is neither the time nor the place to ask that particular question.

Since Keith always arrives at the hall in the same clothes he wears onstage, the good news is that no one will have to wait for him to select an outfit in which to perform this evening. As Keith charges into the next room to find his guitar, Anita sinks into a chair across from Mick and Bianca while balancing Marlon on her lap. Essentially naked tonight in a skimpy pair of silver lamé hot pants and a black push-up bra over bare skin, she looks every inch like the queen of rock 'n' roll.

Acting as though he now has all the time in the world and nothing better to do, Mick gets Marlon laughing by making funny faces at him. "You been on the road now for eighteen months, Marlon," Mick says. "How do you like this life, eh?"

As soon as Keith appears with a guitar in his hand, the Stones get to their feet and head out the dressing room door. Trailing in their wake, everyone else follows them toward the stage. Decked out this evening in what looks like a coat made from human hair and a see-through blouse, Bianca unwittingly steps in front of Anita as they both head down the hall.

Coming to a dead stop as Bianca keeps right on walking, Anita shoots her a killing look and hisses, "Fuck-eeng bourge-oise cunt voo-man!" Fortunately for all concerned, no one else hears her say this and then at long last, the first show finally begins.

For reasons that may have nothing whatsoever to do with Keith's as yet still unexplained disappearance this afternoon, the Stones do the only truly bad show of the tour. While others have been less than perfect musically, there has always been electricity, excitement, and real contact with the audience. Tonight there is nothing. While the set is not unrepresentative of the music the Stones have been making on the tour and the show might actually be considered a good one by some lesser band, the magic that makes the Rolling Stones so special when they perform onstage simply is not there.

After the show is over, the band gathers in the dressing room for a postmortem that quickly comes to resemble the kind of group therapy session in which none of them would ever willingly participate. Looking even sadder than usual, Bill Wyman sits on the couch staring disconsolately at the floor for so long that Keith finally tells him, "Bill, I'm just saying, don't be so brought down."

"I just want everyone to say it was shit," Bill says. "They queued for five hours and. . . . "

"If you think it's my fault 'cause I missed the train," Keith says, "just say it, Bill."

"I do, yeah," Bill tells him.

Still not exhibiting a shred of guilt about any of this, Keith says, "I was two minutes late at the station. We went to the airport and the jet broke down. Then they brought in a prop and it broke down."

Doing her best to cheer Bill up, Astrid says, "They don't know the difference, Bill. The audience enjoyed themselves. It doesn't matter to them."

Shaking his head stubbornly from side to side, Bill says, "We were shit and you all know it."

Trying to make everyone feel better, Bobby Keys says, "Ah was great. Ah was fantastic. Ah carried y'all." Although a few people smile weakly at the remark, everyone still looks just as grim as they did before.

"It's the house," Keith says. "There's no contact."

Putting an end to the conversation as only he can, Mick says, "I don't care. I don't give a shit. Well, when I'm onstage, maybe. But I'm off now." Reaching out to ruffle Boogie's brown-and-white fur, Mick says, "Right now, I'm petting this little dog here, and that's what I care about." Getting to his feet, he then slowly walks out of the room.

After Mick is gone, Keith looks around the room and says, "Anyone have a joint?"

"Yeah," Gram Parsons says. "Where are the dope dealers when you really need them?"

Sticking his head out of the door, Gram cups both hands around his mouth and yells, "Dope dealers?"

//

Two minutes later as I was making my way up a backstage staircase looking for a bathroom in which I could relieve myself and write down some notes, I nearly stumbled headfirst over Mick Jagger. Looking very much like a lovelorn high school kid, he was sitting on a landing as Bianca held him tightly in her arms. The scene was so intensely personal that all I could do was turn around silently and go right back down the way I had come. So much for Mick Jagger as the devil incarnate or a rock star so utterly jaded that he could not be bothered to care about anything once he was done with it.

For me, this was the night when I realized for the first time just how much the Rolling Stones still really cared about what they were doing. As I would later see proven again and again in the music business, great talent could only take you so far. Right from the start, both Mick and Keith had always shared a laser-like focus on the music. Without it, the Rolling Stones could never have stayed together long enough to be upset about having played one bad show in Liverpool.

And yes, just as I had seen them do in Coventry six nights earlier, the band then went back out onstage for the second show and kicked ass in every way imaginable. At one point, as a skinhead began waltzing an aging usher around in circles and a fifty-five-year-old matron wearing eyeglasses bumped her pelvis obscenely to the beat, Mick Jagger actually found himself standing on top of the piano. It was all great stuff and for the first time on the entire tour the crowd actually applauded Mick Taylor's scorching blues solo in "Love in Vain," which I suppose showed just how really cool the audience in Liverpool still was even in 1971.

Before we leave the city where the Mersey Beat first came spilling into the street from the cellar full of noise on Mathew Street known as the Cavern Club and the Beatles then proceeded to change the face of popular music only to have so recently fallen apart thanks in part to the influence of Linda McCartney and Yoko Ono, the time has come for us to examine what was really going on between Bianca and Anita on this tour.

As Anita herself had so plainly demonstrated while walking toward the stage before the first show, there was absolutely no love lost between her and Bianca. Nor had they liked one another before the tour began. The two women had first met on the night of September 22, 1970, when Bianca came to see the Stones perform at the Palais des Sports in Paris. Standing in the wings in a flowing black cloak, she immediately caught Mick's eye.

As Rose Millar would later say, "I remember when Mick first saw Bianca. She was with Eddie Barclay in Paris and Mick came over to me at the dinner table and said, 'I really like her. But she belongs to somebody else.' And I said, 'Well, that's not going to stop you, is it?' I always thought they were wonderful together. Real foils for one another. She was feisty and had lots of spirit and was very bright. Apparently, she thought I was boring, but I really liked her and thought she was great."

As everyone soon learned, Bianca had absolutely nothing in common with Anita. Then twenty-seven years old, Anita was a former model and actress who had appeared in six films, most notably the shocking and utterly scandalous Performance, in which she not only was frequently naked on screen but also shared a bath with her costars Michele Breton and Mick Jagger, with whom she was then having a torrid on-set affair.

A life artist of the first order who had never paid any attention whatsoever to the rules governing conventional behavior, Anita was a collector and connector of people who by this point in time had already been everywhere, done everything, and knew everyone who mattered in the world of international café society.

Anita's time of service with the Rolling Stones had begun when she met and fell in love with Brian Jones in Munich in 1965. Without her fantastic sense of style and incredible eye for fashion, Brian might never have blossomed into the gender-bending psychedelic peacock he became after the two of them began regularly dropping acid together in their flat in Courtfield Road, which soon became the epicenter of the hippest scene in London.

That Anita left Brian after he had lost all control to be with Keith only made perfect sense because the two of them were so similar in many ways. Much like Keith, Anita was a wild jungle creature whom it seemed no one could ever tame. Like him, she *also did not give a shit what anyone thought of her. At a time when the women's liberation movement was just being born, Anita had already achieved a kind of riotous individual freedom that would eventually lead her as far down the road of excess as anyone had ever gone.*

A magnetic creature who always drew the beautiful people of both sexes to her side, Anita was perfectly suited to live in the world of the Rolling Stones because she thrived on chaos. The crazier things got, the more Anita liked it. Because there was no knowing what might come out of her mouth at any given moment, she could also be as funny as hell.

Before this tour had even begun, the changes wreaked upon Anita's personality by her increasing use of heroin had become apparent to those who knew her well. As Astrid Lundstrom would later say, "I remember being impressed with how strong Anita seemed when she got pregnant with Marlon. When I saw her again at the airport in August 1970 as the Stones were about to go on tour in Europe, I was blown away because she was totally strung out and a mess. She was a mess on the English tour as well, and I think by then she had already lost it in a way."

Despite how loaded Keith and Anita were on the tour, they both still somehow managed to take impeccable care of Marlon without employing a nanny to do any of the dirty work for them. I can still clearly remember Anita laughing and wrinkling her nose at the smell as she leaned toward Marlon in the dressing room in Coventry before the show and said, "Time for a change now, yes?"

Now that we have some sense of who Anita was back then, the reasonable question to ask would be why she and Bianca literally could not stand the sight of one another. From all accounts, the antipathy between them had begun on the 1970 European tour when Anita borrowed some clothes from Bianca only to return them so stained and soiled with God only knows what kind of substances that Bianca refused to ever wear them again.

What was really going on between these two incredibly powerful women back then was a battle for control. Far more than Bianca, who only really cared about Mick, Anita had been the queen bee of the Rolling Stones for so long that she could not bear the thought of anyone taking her throne away. In Astrid Lundstrom's words, "Anita hated Bianca because she took some power away from her. That was the bottom line. And also because, on the surface, Bianca looked like she had it together. Of course, Bianca had enormous influence over Mick as well and that was also something Anita did not like."

Although Beatles' biographer Philip Norman would later call Bianca "the Yoko Ono of the Rolling Stones," the truth is that what really drove Mick Jagger and Keith Richards apart was Keith's increasingly heavy drug use. And while Anita's utter distaste for Bianca certainly did not make things easier for anyone, even Anita knew there was really nothing she could do about Bianca but complain.

For Mick and Keith, the music had always come before the women. And so, despite the way Anita and Bianca felt about one another, the Rolling Stones just went right on making music together on this tour as they had always done before.

CHAPTER EIGHT

LEEDS, MARCH 13, 1971

BEFORE THE FIRST OF TONIGHT'S TWO SHOWS in the refectory of the Student Union Building at the University of Leeds, the Rolling Stones and all those traveling with them sit killing time like students with nothing better to do in the cafeteria. As Mick Taylor tunes up in front of a giant food mixer, Charlie Watts, looking very collegiate in a green-and-white Leeds University sweatshirt, settles down beside Bill Wyman in one of the leatherette booths scattered across an outsized room framed on three sides by huge floor-to-ceiling windows.

Despite how strange the whole scene already seems, things definitely get weirder when Marshall Chess calls everyone's attention to the fact that a horde of desperate fans have assembled right outside the windows. In order to get the Stones to notice them, some of the fans begin slamming their hands against the glass.

Bang-bang-bang and sure enough, one of the windows splinters right down the middle as though it was just struck by a lightning bolt. And while it might seem like a good idea to move those fans back before someone gets seriously hurt, this is still England after all. When a member of the university security staff finally walks into the cafeteria, his solution to the problem is to turn down all the overhead lights so no one can see inside any longer.

As Bianca sits in a booth with her breasts gathered together like a pair of ripe apples beneath a see-through blouse, a bare-chested Mick Jagger begins prancing around with a gold-spangled bolero cape over his shoulders. Wearing far more rouge and lipstick than he has sported before any other show on the tour, Mick looks like the caricature of a rock star he played in *Performance*.

Completely oblivious to everything going on around him, Keith stands all by himself in the middle of the room holding his guitar like it is the only thing anchoring him to the earth. As yet another cloud of smoke from the cigarette he keeps firmly clenched between his front teeth drifts slowly upward, it forms a perfect halo around his head.

With everyone already looking forward to the shows at the Roundhouse in London tomorrow night that will bring the tour to a close, Leeds might be nothing more than just another very strange stop on the road were it not for the fact that some thirteen months ago The Who came here to record what critics on both sides of the Atlantic have already called the greatest live album ever made.

Having always pursued their career with one eye carefully cocked on what every other great band was doing, the Rolling Stones have decided to follow in The Who's footsteps by recording their own live album tonight in Leeds. It is for this reason that the fairly brand-spanking-new, one-of-a-kind mobile recording truck that Ian Stewart assembled with advice from his old friend and former flatmate Glyn Johns is now parked right outside the hall.

While the initial intent behind the project was to enable the Stones to record whenever and wherever they liked without having to pay exorbitant studio fees for sessions at which Mick or Keith did not even appear or the band accomplished almost nothing, what Marshall Chess calls "the rock truck" has now become part of the Stones' new overall business plan.

Packed to the rafters with £100,000 ($240,000) worth of sixteen-track recording equipment and painted a sickening shade of khaki green for what Marshall calls "camouflage," the truck has already been used to record several tracks for *Sticky Fingers* at Stargroves, Mick Jagger's palatial estate in the English countryside.

To continue recouping their sizable investment in the truck, Marshall says the Stones will be leasing it out to other bands for £1,500 ($3,600) a week. And since Mick will no longer be living there once the Stones decamp to France, Stargroves is being outfitted as a state-of-the-art, live-in recording studio with round-the-clock facilities that can be rented for £2,500 ($6,000) a week.

Now that the Stones are fully in charge of their own financial affairs for the first time, it only makes eminent sense for them to try to get the maximum return from this tour by recording a live album that might do as well as *Get Yer Ya-Ya's Out!* After being released seven months ago, the album sold a million copies in America and hit the number-one spot on the charts in the United Kingdom.

The man who recorded, produced, and mixed that album will be sitting behind the board in the rock truck tonight. A longtime member in good standing of the band's extended family, Glyn Johns began his career with the Rolling Stones by recording their first demo tracks at IBC Studios in London in 1963. More recently, he also engineered some of the sessions that the Stones did at Olympic Studios for *Sticky Fingers.*

A tall, lean man with dark hair and sharp cheekbones who is making a definite fashion statement tonight in black leather pants and a red wet leather jacket with a white fur collar, Glyn slowly begins working his way across the cafeteria in search of something to drink before the first show begins. Much like his great friend Ian Stewart, Glyn is one of the few people around the Rolling Stones who never minces words in describing how the band has always gone about making records in the studio.

///

Long after his time of service with them was done, Glyn Johns would note that the Rolling Stones had no idea what a record producer actually did because until Jimmy Miller came along, the band had never had one. Born in Brooklyn, Miller was a talented drummer who had begun his producing career with the Spencer Davis Group, for whom he had also cowritten the hit single "I'm a Man" with Stevie Winwood.

Impressed by the work that Miller was doing with Traffic in the next room at Olympic Studios while the Stones were recording Their Satanic Majesties Request, *Glyn Johns urged Mick Jagger to hire Miller to produce the band's next album. A quantum leap from their previous work in the studio,* Beggars Banquet *was Miller's first effort with the Stones and it became a huge success, both critically and commercially.*

As Glyn Johns would later say, "The Rolling Stones, that is to say Mick and Keith, were incredibly difficult to produce. I mean, how do you tell Keith Richards that what he just played wasn't any good? Actually, you don't. I once made the mistake of telling Keith he was out of tune and you would have thought I had just told him his mother was a whore."

Not surprisingly, the key to Miller's success with the Rolling Stones was his working relationship with Keith Richards. As Glyn Johns's younger brother Andy would later say, *"Jimmy came in and pulled the Stones together and turned them back into more of a proper rock 'n' roll band than they had ever really been before. He did* Beggars Banquet, *which was fucking brilliant, and then* Let It Bleed, *which was bloody marvelous.*

"When it came to playing grooves, Jimmy was the instigator. On 'Honky Tonk Women,' he went out into the studio and started playing two little cowbells, one atop of another on a steel prong, and set the tempo for the whole song. Jimmy really knew how to get fantastic grooves and come up with cool sounds and during the late sixties and early seventies, he was seen as quite a magician in the studio."

Even with Jimmy Miller behind the board in the studio, Keith Richards continued to be just as unpredictable as ever when it came to showing up on time for a session. As Glyn Johns would later say, *"While we were making* Let It Bleed, *there were many occasions when we would work without Keith because he wasn't there. It would be three or four in the morning and as we would be getting in the car to go home, Keith would arrive and everyone would troop back in like they were in his employ or something. I remember waiting for Keith for three days in Hamburg and he never came and nobody got annoyed. They just accepted it.*

"If you want to talk about someone in the band being indulged, it was not Mick. Keith got the Oscar. This was somebody from

the outside looking in who did not give a monkey's bum about anybody. Underneath all that, Keith could be an extremely loving, caring, considerate person. There were people he cared about that he would die for. And Ian Stewart was one of them. But in the main, Keith's general reaction with anybody he was working with or who was around him was that he couldn't care less about them. They didn't enter into it because he just didn't care.

"The most frustrating thing to me was when the Stones would sit and play a track for hours and hours and hours, the same thing over and over again. At the beginning, it would sound fantastic. It had all the spark and the adrenaline. After three days, it was deadening and awful. Everyone thinks the Rolling Stones made pretty amazing records. I can assure you they could have been and actually were at one point fifty times better than they ended up being, at least from a rhythm track point of view. By the time they got the track that Keith liked, they were all worn out or played out. Because by then his part had developed into what he wanted."

Already working constantly with so many other artists that his patience with the chaos that always ensued when the Rolling Stones went into the studio had just about come to an end, Glyn Johns was about to be supplanted as the band's engineer of choice by his younger brother Andy. Unlike Glyn, who aside from Ian Stewart and Jo Bergman was the only person around the Stones who was completely straight, Andy Johns would soon become so deeply involved in drugs with Keith and Jimmy Miller that his life would never be the same.

///

In what was meant to serve as a dry run for tonight's effort, Glyn was also behind the board of the rock truck as it sat parked outside the Empire Theatre last night in Liverpool so he could record both of those shows as well. Taking a quick look around the room to make sure neither Mick nor Keith is listening, Glyn sighs and says, "I hope they play better tonight than last. I really do." Spinning on his heel, Glyn Johns then walks out the door to begin what will be one of the last nights he will ever work for the Rolling Stones.

///

Mad as it may seem in this day and age of carefully planned marketing and digital media campaigns designed to sell new albums through every means available to man, the Rolling Stones were touring Great Britain a month before Sticky Fingers *was to be released. Although the Stones had no real choice in the matter because they had to be out of the country by April 1 for tax reasons, they did find themselves playing as many as four or five songs from the new album each night that no one in the audience had ever heard.*

By this point in the tour, I had seen the band perform "Bitch" and "Brown Sugar" so many times that both songs had burned their way into my brain. Unfortunately, this was also the only place I could hear them once the night's shows were over. Utterly possessed by those pounding horn parts and Keith's unrelenting rhythm guitar riffs, I would walk around all day long singing as many of the lyrics as I could remember over and over to myself.

Even though the album was not yet out, Marshall Chess was God's own salesman when it came to pushing it to all the eager record buyers who then made up the core readership of Rolling Stone magazine. As Marshall was only too happy to tell me, the ten tracks on Sticky Fingers *were (in what would turn out not to* be the final running order) "Bitch," "Brown Sugar," "You Gotta Move," "Dead Flowers," "I Got the Blues," "Sister Morphine," "Keep-a-Knockin'" (i.e., "Can't You Hear Me Knocking"), "Wild Horses," "Sway," and "Moonlight Mile."

Befitting the utterly chaotic way in which the Rolling Stones recorded back then, Marshall said that even though the album was slated to be released during the third week in April, there was still a chance Mick might want to go back into the studio to re-record some of his vocals. Because he literally did not have the time to do this once the tour was over, this never happened. But to have even been considering the possibility after having spent more than a year in the studio at a cost of £42,000 (a little less than $100,000) spoke volumes about just how difficult it was for Mick and Keith to ever let go of an album that everyone else thought was long since done.

Because I was still completely clueless about the economics of the music business back then, what I did not understand was just how badly the Rolling Stones needed their new album to be a hit. Throughout the entire tour as the band played their asses off onstage night after night, the elephant in the room was whether or not Sticky Fingers would sell enough copies to justify the insanely lucrative deal that Ahmet Ertegun had given the Stones so he could distribute their next five albums.

As difficult as this may now also be to understand, the Rolling Stones were not yet the heavyweight champions of record sales they have since become. After being released in December 1968, Beggars Banquet had gone platinum in America by selling a million copies. A year later, Let It Bleed had sold twice as many records and gone double platinum. Reverting to form, Get Yer

Ya-Ya's Out! *had sold a million copies in America after being released in September 1970.*

While these sales figures were certainly nothing to be ashamed of and continued to provide Mick and Keith with a steady source of income as songwriters thanks to the deal they had signed with Decca Records, the totals paled in comparison to the number of albums that bands like Chicago, Santana, and Blood, Sweat, and Tears were then selling. Released just six weeks before the Stones' tour began, Simon and Garfunkel's Bridge over Troubled Water *was on its way to going eight times platinum in America while selling an astonishing 25 million copies worldwide.*

It had been for precisely this reason that Clive Davis, then the head of Columbia Records, decided to pass on signing the Stones to his label. In the end, the only record company suitor willing to meet Stones' business manager Prince Rupert Loewenstein's demand for a huge advance as well as what Davis called "a staggering royalty rate" was Atlantic Records. Obsessed with not just the music of the Rolling Stones but Mick Jagger as well, Ahmet Ertegun pursued the band for more than a year and then agreed to come up with a $1 million advance for each of their next five albums against what was then the unprecedented royalty rate of 10 percent.

Further complicating the upcoming release of Sticky Fingers *was what both Mick and Keith saw as a deliberate act of corporate pique as well as an attempt to extract one last return on its initial investment in the band. On March 6, 1971, Decca Records issued a compilation of Stones' tracks recorded in the mid-1960s that had never before appeared on an album in the United Kingdom. Aptly entitled* Stone Age, *the cover of the album featured a weathered* stone wall on which graffiti relating to the Rolling Stones had been scrawled.

Adding further insult to injury, the artwork was a total rip-off of the far superior image of a graffiti-covered bathroom wall complete with open toilet that Decca had refused to allow the Stones to use as the cover for Beggars Banquet, *thereby delaying the release of that album for several months. Without fully understanding the irony of his remark as he spoke about it in the dressing room before a show one night, Mick described what Decca had done as trying to get "blood from a stone."*

Of course by then Mick had already pissed the label off no end by cutting a song entitled "Schoolboy Blues" that in time would come to be known as "Cocksucker Blues" as the Stones' final single for Decca. Having refused for good reason to release the track, the company was now just paying Mick and the Stones back in kind for having decided to leave Decca to form a label of their own.

Six days after the tour was over, the Stones took out full-page ads in the English pop press stating, "We didn't know this record was going to be released. It is, in our opinion, below the standard we try to keep up, both in choice of content and cover design." Despite the ads, Stone Age *went to number four on the album charts in the United Kingdom. While the record business had already become far more corporate than it had ever been before, the entire contretemps spoke volumes about how truly vile and disgusting the industry could still be even at the very highest levels of the game.*

In the end, the good news was that the very expensive corporate gamble Ahmet Ertegun had taken on the future of the Rolling Stones paid off handsomely for all concerned. In May

1971, *the first single from* Sticky Fingers, *"Brown Sugar"—a song inspired by backup singer Claudia Lennear that Mick Jagger had originally wanted to call "Black Pussy"—went to number one on the charts in America.*

On May 22, 1971, Sticky Fingers *replaced Crosby, Stills, Nash, & Young's live* 4 Way Street *album at number one on the Billboard charts. Staying there for three weeks, it eventually became the most commercially successful album the Rolling Stones had ever made by selling three million copies in America while also doing far better worldwide than any of the band's previous efforts.*

Because Mick and Keith had written and recorded several of the tracks on Sticky Fingers *while they were still under contract to Allen Klein, the bad news was that he owned the copyrights to those songs. Although neither Mick nor Keith earned the far more lucrative royalties that Atlantic would have paid them, all they had to do to make up for that was begin writing and recording brand-new material for what was now their eagerly awaited second album on Rolling Stones Records. As all those faithful readers who have made their way through* Exile on Main St.: A Season in Hell with the Rolling Stones *already know, this would prove to be a story of an entirely different cloth.*

Nonetheless, the answer to the question that had been lurking in the back of everyone's mind during the entire tour as to whether the Rolling Stones' new album would be a big success was a resounding yes. Against all odds and with the deck stacked firmly against them, Sticky Fingers *would make it possible for the Rolling Stones to begin the next chapter in their career.*

And what of the live album Glyn Johns had come to Leeds to record in the rock truck that was Ian Stewart's pride and joy?

Alternately called Live in Leeds *or* Get Your Leeds Lungs Out, *it is currently available in bootleg form all over the Internet and has also been streamed on the BBC Radio 6 website. While you can hear what the Stones sounded like onstage back then, it pales in comparison to how good they were live. Insofar as I can tell from my notes, neither of the shows in Leeds that night impressed me as being anything very special. Which was probably the reason the Stones decided to forget about following in the footsteps of The Who.*

///

As always in Leeds tonight, "Midnight Rambler" is the highlight of both shows. At one point, as Mick croons, "Go down on me, bay-bee," he actually looks out into the house to see if anyone is hip enough to get what he is singing about. As Mick does this, the stage lights hit the gold spangles on his cape at an angle that makes the reflection shoot all the way up to the perforated white tile ceiling. For the rest of the song, tiny bursts of light swim around in circles high above Mick's head like a school of crazy fish.

Before "Midnight Rambler" comes to an end, the lady who has been traveling with trumpeter Jim Price throughout the entire tour very politely throws up twice at the side of the stage and then walks off quietly down the hall to the dressing room. So much for Leeds. And now, on to London.

CHAPTER NINE

LONDON, MARCH 14, 1971

AT LONG LAST, A GIG THAT REALLY MATTERS. On Sunday in London, everyone lucky enough to get their hands on a ticket to see the Rolling Stones washes their hair and then stands in the long, curling line that winds its way around the Roundhouse on Chalk Farm Road.

Originally built to serve as a railway engine turntable shed, the massive circular concrete structure is a unique and unbelievably funky venue where members in good standing of the London underground regularly assemble to fill the air with fuming clouds of hash smoke as they watch bands like Hawkwind and the Pink Fairies perform at deejay Jeff Dexter's regular Sunday night concert series known as "Implosion."

When the Stones last played here in London at the Saville Theatre and the Lyceum in the West End in December 1969, they performed before an audience of what Dexter would later call "the Chelsea elite." As anyone can plainly see, tonight's crowd bears no resemblance whatsoever to that particular aspect of London society.

Looking as though the Sheriff of Nottingham just evicted them all from Sherwood Forest, a horde of long-haired freaks of both sexes decked out in fringed buckskin, dark green velvet, and hand-crocheted cloaks of many colors comes streaming toward the hall from the Chalk Farm Tube stop across the road. Ignoring the scalpers who are now working the street for all they are worth by quoting prices no one can afford, those who have already paid for their tickets slowly make their way toward the portal that leads into the Roundhouse.

Outside the backstage door where only those whose names have been written down by hand on the guest list will be permitted to enter, an entirely different scene is taking place. Because this is London and these are the Rolling Stones, a multitude of music business luminaries as well as the crème de la crème of the underground have turned out in force to see these shows. Unaccustomed to ever having to stand in line at any gig, they also wait patiently to be allowed inside the hall.

Backstage, a freak show of major proportions is under way. Packed in so tightly that they might as well be standing on the Tube during rush hour, forty-two people jam the Stones' dressing room. As Mick eyes a lady with henna hair who looks pretty much naked down the front, one very formidable-looking black man with a huge Afro passes a joint to another and says, "Are you black, man?"

Because someone has come up with the bright idea of keeping the cold water in the showers running full blast so all the cans of beer and soda will not get warm, the roaring sound makes it just that much harder to hear what anyone is saying. Bottles of tequila and bowls of sliced lemons, bananas, nuts, and raisins line a table

Mick and Bianca arriving in Newcastle for the first show of the tour.
CREDIT: Mirrorpix Archive.

Bill Wyman and Astrid Lundstrom leaving the train in Newcastle with Charlie Watts directly behind them.
CREDIT: Mirrorpix Archive.

Chip Monck and Charlie Watts. *CREDIT:* Nevis Cameron, Chipmonck Archive.

Chip Monck and his crew erecting the light truss in Newcastle City Hall. *CREDIT:* Nevis Cameron, Chipmonck Archive.

Keith, Marlon, and Anita leaving the hotel in Newcastle. *CREDIT:* Mirror-pix Archive.

As your correspondent looks on from the left, Nicky Hopkins, Jim Price, Mick Taylor, and Rose Millar leave the hotel in Newcastle. *CREDIT:* Mirrorpix Archive.

Mick on stage
in Manchester.
CREDIT: Mirrorpix
Archive.

Rose Millar,
baby Chloe, and
Mick Taylor.
CREDIT: Mirrorpix
Archive.

Gram Parsons, mistakenly identified as Donovan for lo these many years in the *Daily Mirror* archive. *CREDIT:* Mirrorpix Archive.

Keith in Coventry with Boogie in hand. *CREDIT:* Mirrorpix Archive.

Keith on stage in Liverpool. *CREDIT:* Mirrorpix Archive.

The Stones on stage in Leeds with Bobby Keys and Jim Price. *CREDIT:* Nevis Cameron, Chipmonck Archive.

Ian Stewart with Mick. *CREDIT:* Out-Take Ltd.

against the wall but the scene is such a groupie's who's who of rock in London circa 1971 that no one can be bothered to eat or drink a thing.

Looking very cool in a dark green velvet jacket, Traffic lead guitarist Dave Mason stands talking to ex–Mad Dogs and Englishmen drummers Jim Gordon and Jim Keltner. Out in the hallway where various members of Family, the Edgar Broughton Band, and the Faces are hanging out, some girl no one knows suddenly passes out and Ian Stewart has to carry her past all the musicians into the Stones' dressing room so she can be revived.

Upstairs, legendary disc jockeys Tom Donahue, who has come to England to interview Mick for a promotional LP that will be distributed to radio stations all over America, and John Peel, who will soon be given an hour-long tape of the Stones' show in Leeds to broadcast on his popular BBC Radio 1 show, jockey for elbow room in the unbelievably crowded balcony. Gathered around them tonight is the entire English pop press, a good deal of the English straight press, a gaggle of thoroughly wired rock 'n' roll PR people, a clutch of high-powered record executives, and a collection of incredibly well-dressed upper-class hippies, all of whom look as though they have never done an honest day's work in their lives.

A dead ringer for Daisy Callahan as she sits in front of a mirror in the Stones' dressing room in a cloche hat decorated with green peacock feathers, a floral skirt, and an outrageous black ostrich feather jacket, Bianca smokes a cigarette from an ivory holder that has to be at least eight inches long. Calmly minding her own business, she watches as Mick asks Gram Parsons if he can borrow his belt to wear onstage tonight because he has forgotten his own.

As though she was born to pop stardom and has every right in the world to be here tonight, Joyce the Voice, whose trip it is to be all trippy and sometimes walk out onstage to grab the microphone for unscheduled raps no one wants to hear, suddenly appears before the mirror. Talking directly to Bianca, she says, "Excuse me, but didn't I see you with Osibisa in their dressing room last week?"

What? What is this? I mean, hold on. Joyce the Voice has just asked Bianca, she of the inscrutable face, blinding smile, mysterious eyes, and gin rummy ways, Joyce has just asked Mick Jagger's lady, "Excuse me, but aren't you a groupie for this band I know?"

Although the question deserves no response, Bianca is nothing if not polite and so says, "What is Osibisa?"

"Oh wow," Joyce says with a completely straight face, not knowing she has just been cut dead and left lying face down on the dressing room floor. "There is someone with your exact vibration around. I mean, like a twin sister. You know? Someone who is walking around with your face."

As Bianca rolls her eyes upward, Joyce is promptly escorted out the door. Slowly working his way across the room, a skinny old man holding a sheet of paper in his hand comes up to Mick and says, "Who's Mick Jagger now? It's not for me. It's an autograph for a little girl, a spastic she is, no legs neither. C'mon now. You *are* in the group, ain't ya?"

And while you might think Mick would waste no time having this old man shown the door as well, he very softly says, "Yeah, I am," and then signs his name on the sheet of paper. "Should I steer you to the others?" Mick asks. "That's Charlie right over there."

Out in the hallway, someone is trying to get Gram Parsons to sign a record contract. As all the people who have only just been thrown out of the Stones' dressing room file past him on their way into the hall, Gram casts a baleful eye in their direction and says, "Après moi, le déluge."

Proving that Gram definitely knows of what he speaks, the Stones come rushing right by him a moment later on their way to the stage. While the first show of the night leaves nothing to be desired, it does not come close to meeting the expectations of those who have been waiting to see this gig since tickets first went on sale more than a month ago. For this, no one can blame the Stones. The audience is just so super-hip and spaced out that people dance only because they think this is what they are supposed to do.

Although the scene backstage between shows is far quieter than it was before, the kind of high-society buzz that could be found nowhere else on the tour is still going around the dressing room. As joints are passed, shots of tequila knocked back, and cocaine sniffed from tiny silver spoons, neither Mick nor Keith seems in any hurry for this party to end.

Going onstage an hour late for the second show, the Stones power their way through a tough set during which the microphones suddenly go dead in the middle of "Street Fighting Man." To celebrate the end of the tour and amuse himself as well as the Stones and the audience, Chip Monck has assigned a member of his crew to sit at the very edge of the balcony holding a string fastened to the plywood top of a large canvas hamper. As the show nears the end, Chip cues the guy to pull the string. The plywood top swings open and from the hamper come thousands of ping-pong balls painted in bright fluorescent colors.

Cascading down through shafts of light, the ping-pong balls nearly bury Mick as he stands at the very edge of the stage. Doubling up with laughter, Mick actually stops singing for a moment. Far too busy trying to grab the ping-pong balls that are now bouncing crazily in every direction so they can take them home as souvenirs, no one in the crowd seems to notice.

As yellow flowers and white confetti fly around the stage, Mick and Keith celebrate by swigging champagne straight from the bottle. Since the Tube in London shuts down at eleven-thirty on Sunday night and this is the way most of those here tonight will be going home, the Rolling Stones leave the stage for the final time on their farewell tour of England at the stroke of eleven.

Filing out into the damp and foggy night through the wide-open doors of the Roundhouse, the crowd begins heading off down Chalk Farm Road. Behind them, they leave the smell of stale sweat and hash smoke and patchouli as well as the empty stage on which the Rolling Stones just performed. Having already left the building, they have no expectations to ever pass through here again.

///

For the world's greatest rock 'n' roll band, an era had just come to an end. Never again would the Rolling Stones board trains and buses to play two shows a night in aging city halls and theaters that could only accommodate 2,000 people. Like a hydra-headed monster no one could control, the music business was about to expand so exponentially that in just a few years' time it would bear no relationship to what it had once been.

As always, the Rolling Stones were right at the forefront of this revolution. And so when the band returned to London in 1976, they performed at Earl's Court with the kind of over-the-top production that was required to entertain the audience in such a massive venue.

At the Roundhouse on the final night of the tour, there were no fabulous special effects, no light show, and no larger-than-life video screens. The Stones were just a great band playing onstage. And even though many of those in the audience that night had come there to see and be seen rather than just lose themselves in the music, there were moments when the joint was really rocking and going round and round.

Before bidding a fond farewell to the Roundhouse, I feel compelled to detail what I can only describe as my very own moment of truth with Mick Jagger. As I stood in the dressing room between shows that night wondering how long it was going to take me to write my piece about the tour, Mick came up to me for what I thought would be just another friendly little chat.

Leaning forward until his face was just inches from mine, he flashed me a truly chilling smile and said, "You've been as stoned as anyone on this tour, haven't you?" Not about to deny the obvious, I just laughed and said, "Yeah, well, I guess that could be true."

Continuing to pursue this line of inquiry like a prosecutor at the Old Bailey, Mick said, "You haven't even taken a single bloody note, have you?"

While I could have told Mick about all the time I had spent during the previous ten days writing down everything I had seen and heard in freezing cold and unbelievably filthy lavatories all over England, I just laughed again and mumbled a reply so thoroughly incoherent that it does not bear repeating here. Sneering at me like I had just proven his point beyond any shadow of a doubt,

Mick said, "The real truth is—you've got no bloody idea at all what's happened on this tour, have you?"

Had I been someone other than a fairly clueless rock journalist trying to claw his way to fame and fortune on the backs of the Rolling Stones, I could have said, "Mick, what about that village in Bali where people stay up all night listening to concerts you said we were going to rap about? Can't we talk about that now instead?" Instead, I just stood there without uttering a single word in my own defense.

Because Mick could not have cared less about what kind of article I was going to write concerning the tour, I now know that nothing I might have said to him back then would have made the slightest bit of difference. What Mick was really doing was rattling my cage and jangling my chain as loudly as possible so he could see how I would react. On some level, none of it was even personal.

At some point, nearly everyone who had not been around the Rolling Stones since the beginning had to pass through Mick Jagger's burning ring of fire. If you did, then you were worthy and could continue your association with the band. If you failed Mick's test, then the Stones would just move on without you as they had already done with more people than anyone could name.

Based on Mick's completely one-sided conversation with me in the dressing room at the Roundhouse between shows, there was no doubt in my mind as to which side of that line I was now on. As I trudged back up Haverstock Hill to my flat that night, I knew my brief career with the Rolling Stones had just come to a sudden end.

CHAPTER TEN

THE MARQUEE, MARCH 26, 1971

POOR KEITH. SAY WHAT YOU WILL about the man but ever since the tour ended twelve days ago, his life has pretty much been what even he might describe as a living hell. Leaving London on the day after the final two shows at the Roundhouse, Keith headed straight for Redlands, his country estate in West Sussex. And while no one could deny he had certainly earned the right to enjoy some peace and quiet before going into tax exile in the South of France, Keith had a far more urgent problem to solve before he could even begin to think about this.

Because he and Anita were shooting as much as a third of a gram of heroin a day during the tour, neither of them can leave the country without first undergoing some form of treatment to clean themselves up. And so instead of taking long, bracing walks through the woods at Redlands, Keith lies in bed twitching and puking as he endures the same nightmare of a cure that did not keep either him or Gram Parsons straight for long just a month ago.

A day after Keith starts kicking, Anita admits herself to Bowden House, an exclusive private nursing facility in North

London where only those with money can afford to go. Because she has regularly been skin-popping cocaine and heroin speedballs, Anita is even more strung out than Keith and so is given sleeping pills and methadone to help her through the agony of withdrawal.

Emerging from his own hellish cure looking somewhat pale and battered but otherwise none the worse for wear, Keith returns to London on the day before the Stones are scheduled to appear at the Marquee Club on Wardour Street in the West End. Although the sole purpose of this gig is to film the band in performance for a television special, gaining admission to see the Stones perform in the club on Friday night has promptly become the hottest ticket in town.

To ensure that all those on the band's guest list will be admitted without any hassles, Stones' publicity director Les Perrin asks Chip Monck to come up with a set of special passes for the event. Taking an image supplied to him by designer John Pasche, Monck prints it out onto fifty small self-adhesive patches with the words NOT RECOMMENDED FOR APPLICATION ON SUEDE OR VELVET on the back. "And that was how the tongue logo was born," Monck would later say. "The first time anyone saw it was as the pass for the Stones' show at the Marquee Club."

The first of what will prove to be an endless series of problems at the Marquee occurs as soon as the crew starts loading in the gear. Getting right into it with Chip Monck, the director of the television special informs him that he needs at least 600 foot-candles of light onstage to be able to film the Stones. Although Monck does his best to satisfy this demand, neither man seems all that pleased with the end result.

Just as they have done so many times before, the Rolling Stones spend the afternoon waiting for Keith Richards to arrive. Looking, as Bill Wyman will later write, "awful, dirty, unshaven, and very untogether," Keith finally shows up four hours late in a mood too foul for anyone to ignore. Being Keith, he does not bother to explain why he feels this way.

As though everything he has been going through lately is not enough, Keith stepped out of the front door of his very fashionable town house on Cheyne Walk today only to be surrounded by a brace of policemen. In the unctuous manner that English coppers always use when addressing someone they want to arrest on sight, they said, "Hello, Keith. How are you, boy? Let's roll up your sleeve, eh? Let us have a look at your veins. Not on the heavy stuff, are you? How's Anita and the baby? What's this? Does this smell like hash to you, Fred?"

From their point of view, it all makes perfect sense. Knowing Keith is about to escape their clutches for good by fleeing to the South of France, the cops would love to pin one final bust on him before he goes. Having gone through all this before with Brian Jones, and then at Redlands, and then when both Mick and Marianne Faithfull were busted in Mick's house right next door, what really freaks Keith out is that some detective sergeant eager for a payoff or a promotion might not think twice about planting something on him.

As Keith will later say, referring to the £7,000 in bribes Mick paid to make the Redlands bust go away to no avail, "At least in the States you know the cops are bent and if you want to get into it, you can go to them and say, 'How much do you want?' But in

England, you can drop fifty grand and the next week they'll still bust you and say, 'Oh, it went to the wrong hands. I'm sorry. It didn't get to the right man.' It's insane."

Still suffering the aftereffects of his recent bout with heroin withdrawal, Keith can now no longer even leave his house without being rousted by the law. And if that were not enough, Keith has only just learned that Anita is having so much trouble trying to kick in Bowden House that she will not be able to accompany him and Marlon to France. With the weight of the world now squarely upon his shoulders, is it any wonder the man has no patience at all for what is now going on at the Marquee?

As trumpeter Jim Price will later say, "The Marquee was a big disaster. There were a lot of arguments going back and forth between the band and Mick and Keith and the club owner and the director of the film. There was no role for Bobby Keys or me to play but there were a lot of delays and we were there all day long and did practically nothing."

By now, anyone who has ever seen Keith in action when the darkness is upon him should know there is no way in the world this show will proceed without a hitch. In this case, the hitch is presented by Harold Pendleton, the former accountant and well-known jazz buff who first began putting on shows at the Marquee when it was still located at 165 Oxford Street.

Featuring Mick Jagger on vocals and harmonica, Keith Richards and Elmo Lewis (aka Brian Jones) on guitars, Dick Taylor on bass, Ian Stewart on piano, and Mick Avory on drums, the Rolling Stones performed for the first time using that name at the Marquee on July 12, 1962. Although Harold Pendleton and the Stones most definitely go all the way back, it is not as though there is any love lost between them. Nor has the band ever performed for Pendleton since then.

Despite all the fairly dark and tangled subtext, none of this would be a problem if someone had not come up with the bright idea of stringing a large banner over the stage that reads THE MARQUEE CLUB, thereby ensuring that it will appear in every frame of the television special. As soon as Mick sees the banner, he demands that it be taken down. Since there will be no show tonight if Mick Jagger decides not to walk out onstage at the Marquee, you might think this would not be an issue.

Because in the business of rock 'n' roll everyone always thinks they are right until someone with more power forces them to change their mind, it turns out in fact to be an issue of major proportions. And so a discussion begins onstage between Mick, Keith, Chip Monck, and Harold Pendleton. Because this is England, no one actually goes so far as to raise his voice but the conversation does soon become quite heated.

As Chip Monck will later say, "Pendleton wanted to hang the Marquee sign over the stage. Yeah, fuck you. We were not at the Newport Folk or Jazz Festival where those words had to be seen behind the artist in every photograph. So I made him take it down. And then I ripped it up. With a big smile on my face. Waiting for the bullets." At some point in the proceedings, Pendleton may have further infuriated the Rolling Stones by muttering, "*Still* shit," behind their backs loudly enough to be overheard.

With all of this as preamble, it should come as no great surprise to anyone that when the Stones finally appear before an audience composed primarily of music business insiders as well as rock luminaries like Jimmy Page, Eric Clapton, Ric Grech, and former Stones' manager Andrew Loog Oldham, Keith rushes over to the side of the stage and swings his guitar at Harold Pendleton's head. As deejay Jeff Dexter, who was there that night, will later say, "Keith just went fucking potty."

Keith will later explain that he did this because, as one of the kingpins of the traditional jazz movement in England, Harold Pendleton had not wanted to see that scene die and so had hated the Stones in their early days. In truth, Keith went after Harold Pendleton that night because he was the only authority figure within range.

While you might think Keith has now vented his frustrations without having blown a fifty-amp fuse, his mental state does not improve as the night wears on. At one point, Mick spends an hour in the dressing room trying to persuade Keith to come back out onstage for the second show. Somehow, the Stones manage to make it through the somewhat abbreviated set that will eventually comprise the television special.

Outside the club, Keith runs into his old friend Michael Cooper, the brilliant photographer who shot the totally psychedelic covers for both *Sgt. Pepper's Lonely Hearts Club Band* and *Their Satanic Majesties Request*. Since Cooper happens to be holding, Keith begins snorting heroin with him. Getting as messed up as only he can, Keith then wanders back into the dressing room only to realize he has lost the keys to his car.

Since the vehicle in question is the beloved dark blue 1966 S3 Bentley Continental Flying Spur known as "Blue Lena" that Keith insists on driving at speeds no human being save for Ian Stewart has ever equaled, this also becomes a minor crisis. As Chip Monck will later say, "Why wouldn't Keith have lost the keys to his car that night? Every now and then, he lost the keys to his life as well."

Although even on his best day, Sherlock Holmes could probably never find something Keith Richards has lost, Alan Dunn, who has worked for Mick Jagger and the Stones since 1968, gets saddled with the task of sorting out this particular problem. After putting Keith in a car that takes him home, Dunn calls the roadside assistance number for the Royal Automobile Club and waits for hours until someone finally shows up at dawn.

As Dunn will later say, "It wasn't all that difficult to bypass the ignition so the Bentley was started and then driven down to Redlands without the keys. The guy who was driving pulled into a field and once the Bentley came to a stop in the mud, that was where the car was left running until it finally ran out of fuel."

Lest anyone think Keith is done raving for the weekend and now intends to focus all his attention on getting ready for the move to France, he is out on the town again the next night. After downing a few margaritas and snorting some cocaine, Keith decides to pay Anita a visit in Bowden House. Leaping into the front seat of a car with Michael Cooper by his side, Keith sets off on what soon becomes a very harrowing twelve-mile journey to Harrow.

Driving as always at top speed, Keith bounces the front wheels of the car off various curbs and passes motorists on the wrong side of the road while honking his horn as loudly as possible to let everyone know he has the right of way. To avoid colliding with a truck as he enters Harrow, Keith whips the steering wheel so suddenly to the side that he crashes the car through an iron fence.

With its front grille now completely crushed, steam shooting out of the radiator, and music from the tape cassette recorder still blasting, the car comes to a dead stop in the middle of a traffic circle. Grabbing all the contraband they have brought with them,

Keith and Michael Cooper decide to make a run for it. Heading just as fast as they can away from the scene of the crime, they go through a gate into a quiet English garden. As they begin digging a hole in the ground in which to hide their stash, the door to the house suddenly swings opens and out steps Nicky Hopkins. Politely, he asks them in for tea.

Going inside, Keith and Michael Cooper tend to their cuts and bruises as Nicky phones for a limo to take them to Bowden House. When Keith calls Anita to tell her what happened, she screams hysterically at him, "Just get me some H or I'm checking out of here right now. This minute!"

Leaving the facility the next day so she can score some heroin, Anita returns to Bowden House only to then begin snorting cocaine. At some point, a doctor who is on staff there informs Keith that Anita now has more drugs in her system than when she first entered the facility. Seemingly unable to kick any other way, Anita undergoes what was then known as "the sleeping cure." After being heavily sedated for a week, she finally manages to withdraw from heroin.

A month after Keith and Marlon have left England, Anita joins them in the South of France during the first week in May. With the English tour having long since faded in everyone's memory, the Rolling Stones are now about to start what they believe will be a bright and shiny brand-new chapter in their career. And so it will. What no one in the band understands is how great a price each of them will have to pay to make this happen.

CHAPTER ELEVEN

MAIDENHEAD, MARCH 30, 1971

WHAT BETTER WAY TO WASH AWAY THE BAD TASTE that the fiasco at the Marquee Club has left in everyone's mouth than by swilling as much champagne as possible at a party to which the Rolling Stones have invited a very select group of friends to help them bid farewell to the land of their birth. Adding to the allure, the gala will be taking place in a rather fashionable small hotel on the banks of the River Thames.

Just forty minutes by train from London's Paddington Station, Skindles Hotel in Maidenhead sits right on the river by a very picturesque stone bridge. Although both Winston Churchill and Princess Margaret have stayed at Skindles in the past, the hotel has also earned itself a somewhat notorious reputation as the place where those engaged in adulterous affairs in London often go to have it off with one another in relative privacy.

The Rolling Stones will be spending their last night together in England there because Lady Elizabeth Anson has determined that Skindles is the perfect site for this particular celebration. Having spent the last eleven years putting on gala parties virtually every night of the week for those who can afford her services, Lady Elizabeth is not only really good at what she does but also a cousin of the Queen and the younger sister of one of Mick's good friends, the well-known photographer Patrick Lichfield.

As Lady Elizabeth will later say, "Mick himself seemed to really care about the details. He explained to me that because the party might get out of control, we didn't really want to have it in a historically listed building or some place with a fine collection of art where if people decided to trash things, we would get ourselves in deep trouble.

"And so I began thinking along the lines of 'Where can I find somebody who is pretty desperate and would like the notoriety of having such a party because of the business it would bring them and won't mind terribly if a bit of trashing goes on?' Skindles was going through a very, very tough time financially, and so they were very pleased indeed to have the rental."

After Jo Bergman goes to check out the place, she decides that, yes indeed, this is where the party should take place. Leaving all the details to Lady Elizabeth and her staff, Jo then turns her focus to a problem Marshall Chess has only just brought to her attention.

As Jerry Pompili, who worked as the house manager of the Fillmore East in New York before doing security for the Stones on the English tour, will later say, "Although *Sticky Fingers* had not yet been released, someone suddenly realized no one had ever bothered to write down the lyrics for 'Bitch,' 'Brown Sugar,' 'Moonlight Mile,' and 'Can't You Hear Me Knocking,' which meant that those four songs could not be copyrighted. Jo Bergman had me go over to Mick's house with the acetates and drop a needle on them and try to figure out what the hell he was singing. Which was not really all that easy.

"I played the acetates over and over and wrote down all the lyrics I could understand by hand. Then I took the pages back to Jo and Mick came into the office and looked at them and that got his memory going so he was able to fill in most of the blanks. We had one disagreement and it was on 'Can't You Hear Me Knocking.' There was one line that sounded to me and everybody else like 'Yeah, I've got flatted feet now, now, now,' but Mick swore that was not what he had sung. He couldn't remember what it was, so we just went with 'Yeah, I've got flatted feet now, now, now.'"

A very tough and savvy street guy from New Jersey who often carried a Beretta in his back pocket while on duty at the Fillmore East, Pompili then begins working with Lady Elizabeth Anson on planning the party. Ignoring the fact that the two of them are as different as chalk and cheese, Pompili also begins hitting on her but to no avail. Apparently recognizing his true talents, Lady Elizabeth assigns Pompili the all-important task of setting off the fireworks display that will serve as one of the highlights of the Stones' farewell party on the banks of the Thames.

With vintage champagne flowing freely from the bar, two hundred people crowd a ballroom where weddings and tea dances are usually held. Although John Lennon, Yoko Ono, Eric Clapton, Roger Daltrey, and Stephen Stills are all there, Keith Richards is nowhere to be seen. Considering the wild spirit of abandon everyone seems to have brought with them to this party tonight, this will in the end prove to be a blessing in disguise for all concerned.

As loud music plays over the public address system, people begin getting royally pissed. As Jerry Pompili will later say, "I don't really remember all that much about the party because just like everyone else who was there, I got extremely fucking drunk. I was totally drenched in champagne, my shirt was off, and I kept trying to corner Elizabeth Anson all night long. Being a proper English lady, she was very polite but I got nowhere with her at all.

"At one point in the evening, I stumbled down to the banks of the river where the fireworks were so we could begin shooting them off. I don't know what I was using to ignite them but I set myself on fire and the guy from Chip's crew I had come there with had to roll me in the grass to put out the flames. We were all so fucked up that no one even noticed. I think I must have blacked out after that because the next thing I remember I was sitting in the front seat of my Volkswagen van when John and Yoko came by and said, 'Are you going to London? Can you give us a ride?' And I said, 'Give you a ride? Are you fucking crazy? I can't even stand up.'"

As Lady Elizabeth Anson would later recall, "The guests got ridiculously out of control. That wasn't Mick's idea of fun. It was the hangers-on. I can still clearly remember watching people throwing bottles of vintage champagne into the river and thinking that if anyone at Skindles was really clever, they would send a diver down there after the party and make extra money by recovering the bottles. In fact, I'm sure they're all still there. Right at the bottom of the River Thames."

At around two in the morning, the powers that be at the hotel decide the time has come to shut down the music. Without any warning, the PA suddenly goes dead. Wandering around the ballroom in a somewhat altered state, Bianca starts protesting what has just happened by saying, "You can't do this to us. This is 1971.

Things have progressed beyond this. We can stay up later than two in the morning."

No doubt prompted by how distraught the love of his life feels about this, Mick gets right into it by loudly demanding to know why the music has been stopped. After being told that it was done to comply with a local ordinance, Mick decides to demonstrate his extreme displeasure with this response by flinging a chair through one of the large plate-glass windows overlooking the river.

As Alan Dunn will later say, "I'm not certain if Mick threw that chair through the window because they had shut off the power or as his last act of defiance against the English establishment."

Forget the band's final shows at the Roundhouse or the made-for-television disaster at the Marquee. It is with this signal gesture and the loud sound of breaking glass that the Rolling Stones finally bid farewell to England. Time to turn off the lights. This party is over.

PART TWO

AFTERMATH

///

(In which I finally forsake what by now has become the fairly annoying ploy of using italics to separate myself from who I was back then in order to begin a full-blown account of my time with the Rolling Stones once the English tour was over.)

///

CHAPTER TWELVE

BELFAST, PARIS, AND NICE, MARCH 25–MAY 21, 1971

ONE MONTH AFTER THE TOUR WAS OVER, the 5,300-word article I had written about it appeared in the April 15, 1971, issue of *Rolling Stone* magazine under the title "The Rolling Stones on Tour: Goodbye Great Britain." For those who care about such matters, the cover of that issue featured a photograph of Joe Dallesandro, the underground film star who had made a career out of appearing nude in Andy Warhol films, cradling a naked baby to his bare chest.

In what I suppose you might call a nice bit of synchronicity, it was also Joe Dallesandro whose penis could be seen hanging to the right in a pair of very tight black jeans on the cover designed by Andy Warhol for *Sticky Fingers,* which was released on the very same day. Not that I was thinking about any of this at the time.

For me, the most significant thing about the piece was that I had finally managed to get something I had written published in the back of the magazine rather than on the news pages up front where my articles usually ran. And while no one from the Rolling Stones bothered to get in touch to tell me just how accurately I had portrayed what had happened during the tour, it was not as though I was waiting to hear from them.

Turning my attention to what I thought were definitely far more important stories, I had by then already spent what I can only describe as the single most frightening week of my life in Belfast covering the ongoing religious war between Catholics and Protestants in Northern Ireland colloquially known as "the Troubles."

In a city where everyone was so high on revolution that the sound of automatic weapons fire and bombs going off in the distance at night seemed like music to their ears, I soon realized that unlike Ernest Hemingway, I was not cut out to be a war correspondent and returned to London as quickly as I could.

After I had filed my story about Belfast, I began looking for something new to write about. Without any idea what I was going to do when I got there, I somehow managed to persuade Andrew Bailey, the editor of the London bureau of *Rolling Stone* who had by then also become my good friend, to let me cover the Cannes Film Festival.

On my way there, I stopped off in Paris to interview a high-ranking member of the North Vietnamese delegation to the Peace Talks which had already been going on for years without doing anything to end the war in Vietnam. Not surprisingly, the representative had nothing much new to say and the story never ran. I was about to leave for Cannes when I got a call informing me that I had been chosen to conduct the *Rolling Stone* interview with Keith Richards in the South of France.

After flying to Nice on a prepaid ticket, I walked into an office at the airport to pick up the car someone from London had rented in my name so I could drive to Keith's house to set up the interview. After signing a variety of forms in triplicate, I went back outside only to see that I had been given the keys to a shockingly expensive-looking French sports car. The car was so utterly fabulous that James Bond would not have looked out of place behind the wheel. Unfortunately, I soon discovered that unlike all the cars I had driven in America, this one had a clutch and a stick.

When I tried to exchange the vehicle for something a bit less grand, the woman in the office told me that what with the Cannes Film Festival already in full swing, no other cars were available. My choice was simple. I could either hitch a ride to Keith's house or learn how to drive this sleek machine.

Knowing exactly what James Bond would have done in this situation, I slid suavely behind the wheel of the car, turned the key in the ignition, and stepped down on the gas just as hard as I could. Sputtering loudly, the engine immediately died. Stubbornly, I started it right up again. Again I floored it. Again the engine stalled. After somehow finally managing to jam the stick into first gear, I lifted my foot off the clutch slowly enough to ease out of the parking lot. This was my second big mistake.

Utterly unable to master the intricacies of clutching and shifting, I soon learned I could not even go from first to second without grinding the gears so loudly that the sound was painful to my ears. If I pressed my foot down too hard on the accelerator, the car would shoot forward like a bullet from the barrel of a gun. If I took my foot off the clutch too quickly, the engine would die and the car would stop right in the middle of the road.

Behind me, angry French drivers, all of whom had only recently competed at Le Mans, began to blow their horns. Roaring past me with that classic look of utter Gallic disdain on their faces, motorists of both sexes threw me the French finger while uttering curses that left no doubt as to my dubious parenthood and total lack of brains.

As soon as I reached the stretch of impossibly narrow, curving mountain road high above the sea leading to Villefranche, I knew I was going to die. One false move behind the wheel and I would go careening over the edge and plummet to my death on the jagged rocks far below.

On the spot, I made what I suppose you might call a battlefield decision. No more stopping. From now on, I would not stop for anyone or anything. I would not stop for red lights, I would not stop for stop signs, and I most definitely would not stop for all the gendarmes in blue uniforms who were directing traffic in the middle of crowded roundabouts with whistles clenched between their teeth.

Staying resolutely in second gear as I slowly cruised through one intersection after another, I began waving my hands in crazy circles to let everyone know I was no longer actually in control of this vehicle. For some reason, this technique seemed to work wonders for me and the next thing I knew, I was turning off the treacherous mountain road and on my way to Villefranche.

By the time I finally nosed the car through the massive black wrought-iron front gates of Villa Nellcôte, I was soaked with sweat. Even to myself, I smelled like a dead coyote. My hands were shaking, my self-confidence was shot, and even though the car was somehow still in one piece, I was a total wreck. Having to walk up the broad marble front steps of what looked to me like a smaller version of the Palace at Versailles did nothing to ease my anxiety.

Although I had come to talk to Keith Richards about the *Rolling Stone* interview, I had no idea if he would even know who I was. After all, we had not spoken a single world to one another on the entire tour. While breaking into the dressing room with him in Brighton had been great fun, dropping by unannounced at his palatial home in the South of France was something else again. For all I knew, the man might very well send me packing before I could even begin to explain why I was there.

As I stood waiting in the front hallway for the young French woman who had greeted me to go find "Monsieur Ree-chards," all these thoughts kept churning through my head. Making it all just that much worse, the house was so big that her search seemed to take forever.

And then, without warning, Keith was suddenly standing before me. Looking much healthier and a lot happier than when I had seen him last, he cried out, "Bob Greenfield!" That Keith actually knew my name was an utter shock. This feeling was compounded a hundredfold when Keith stepped forward and hugged me like some long-lost comrade with whom he had soldiered through the war.

As absurd as this may now seem, a feeling of well-being suddenly coursed through my entire body. Like a pilgrim at Lourdes, I had just been cured by the magic healing touch of the star. The great Keith Richards, he of the get-out-of-me-bloody-face-before-I-smash-you-over-the-head-with-me-guitar persona, not only knew who I was but was actually glad to see me.

When Keith said, "So, how are you, man?" I was still so totally blown away that I began to stammer. Regaining my composure, I told Keith I was fine and that it was great to see him but I needed to spend a few days covering the Cannes Film Festival before he and I could start doing the *Rolling Stone* interview together, so would that be cool with him?

With Keith, it was all cool, man. Whenever I was ready, he said I could come back and stay in the house so we could "hang out together and talk and really get this thing done right! Know what I mean, man?" Despite having only a very vague idea of what he was talking about, I told Keith I most certainly did.

Before I knew it, I was back outside the house again and hopping behind the wheel of that car like it had always been my own. With the spirit of 007 coursing through my veins, I turned on the ignition, slid the stick into first, put one foot down on the clutch and the other on the gas, and sped out through the front gates of Villa Nellcôte, spewing gravel behind me in every direction.

Finding my way back to the same twisting stretch of narrow mountain road, I began driving faster than I ever had before while shifting smoothly through all the gears like my brain was now equipped with synchromesh. As I sped past one slowpoke French driver after another, I could not even be bothered to throw them the finger. Instead, I just waved dismissively at them like the great Stirling Moss on his way to yet another Grand Prix win.

When I finally clambered out of the car after arriving in Cannes in world-record time, I was still as high as a kite on an adrenaline rush of major proportions. Although I had never expected this to happen, I was now back in the charmed circle of those who then surrounded the Rolling Stones.

CHAPTER THIRTEEN

VILLA NELLCÔTE I, MAY 27–JUNE 4, 1971

AFTER HAVING SPENT A WEEK fulfilling my lifelong fantasy of attending the Cannes Film Festival, I headed back to Villa Nellcôte where I knew Keith Richards would be waiting to greet me with open arms. After knocking several times on the front door without getting any response, I just took the liberty of letting myself into the house. Calling out Keith's name as softly as I could to announce my presence, I slowly made my way through a huge and completely deserted living room that looked as though it had just been hit by a bomb.

Shipping cartons that had not yet been unpacked stood scattered amid priceless pieces of antique furniture. Along with a good deal of sand, a variety of children's beach toys lay strewn across the very expensive Persian rug covering the polished wooden parquet floor. From the mantle of the ornate white marble fireplace, a ridiculous-looking life-sized cardboard cutout of a shirtless Mick Jagger holding a copy of *Sticky Fingers* over his crotch stood keeping watch over it all.

Stepping through an open doorway into the dining room, I saw Keith sitting at the head of the table. On either side of him were people I did not know. At the far end of the table, Anita was balancing Marlon on her lap. Apparently, everyone had just finished eating lunch. While Keith seemed somewhat pleased to see me, his reaction was nothing compared to the way he had greeted me before.

Although I did not know why, the mood at the table seemed as dark and stormy as the weather had been for the past two weeks in the South of France. Sliding into the nearest empty seat, I did my best to blend into the scenery. As always at Villa Nellcôte, this proved impossible to do.

Turning to me with an inquisitive look on her face, Anita said, "So, did you bring us anything?" Completely misunderstanding her question, I wondered if she was talking about some kind of a housewarming present. Before I could ask, Anita clarified her demand by saying, "Did you bring us anything to smoke?"

Dim as a fifteen-watt lightbulb, I still did not get what she was talking about. Scattered everywhere before me on the table, I could see boxes of Rothman's and Dunhill International cigarettes as well as packets of Gauloises and thick yellow Boyards so powerful that a single puff could knock even the most serious nicotine addict for a loop. If Anita wanted to smoke a cigarette, all she had to do was reach out for one.

Losing all patience with me, Anita said, "Did you bring us something to smoke so we can all get high, yes?" Nodding my head, I said, "Yeah. Actually, I did."

Reaching into the English schoolboy's satchel I carried with me everywhere back then in lieu of a briefcase, I brought forth the little tobacco tin I had been given in Cannes by a long-haired hippie publicity man who did not want to take its contents back with him through customs to America. When Anita opened the lid of the tin and saw all the high-quality Afghani hashish that it contained, her eyes lit up like I had just given her the Christmas present of her dreams.

As though no one else was fit to do the honors, the tin was quickly passed all the way down the table to Keith. From out of nowhere, packets of red Rizla rolling paper suddenly appeared before him. In no time at all, Keith had expertly crumbled just the right amount of black and sticky hash into tobacco from a Rothman's cigarette and created the perfect English joint.

Striking a wooden match against the side of a little box, Keith lit up and inhaled deeply. As he smoked, everyone watched him in utter silence. Was this stuff any good? More to the point, was this stuff good enough for Keith? As the final arbiter in all such matters at Villa Nellcôte, his opinion was the only one that really mattered.

After letting all the smoke back out of his lungs, Keith smiled so broadly that his entire face lit up with delight. Like everything else in this house, the hash was of the highest quality. Although it was purely an accident that I had come there that day bearing tribute, my gift had been accepted in full. Because Keith had given his unqualified seal of approval to what I had brought with me, I was now most definitely persona grata at Villa Nellcôte.

After the joint had been passed around the table several times and smoked down to a glowing roach so that another one had to be rolled and then passed around as well, no one seemed in any hurry to leave. From out of nowhere, several bottles of fine white wine appeared. Drinking and smoking, everyone started telling incredibly funny stories. Before I knew it, the rest of the afternoon slipped away in a pastel-colored haze.

At some point, Keith himself showed me to my room. Located on the far side of the house, it was connected by a door to the room occupied by a man with short dark hair whom Keith and Anita had met while hanging out with the remnants of the Living Theater in Rome. Even though it seemed a bit odd that I had to walk through his room to use the bathroom, we both agreed this would not be a problem for either of us. Because of the man's very active sex life with a variety of local young men, I soon learned that the door was almost always locked.

Bright and early the next morning, I dutifully unpacked my little battery-operated tape recorder and walked out onto the back steps of the house so I could begin interviewing Keith. With his legs crossed beneath him and a newly rolled joint in his hand, he sat without a shirt or shoes basking in the warm sunshine of a perfect spring day in the South of France.

Apparently completely at peace now that he and Anita and Marlon had landed safely in this stately pleasure dome by the sea, Keith never dodged a single question I asked him. Nor did I ever have to prompt him to tell me more. His focus and level of recollection were so extraordinary that a simple question about what he had been doing at art school evoked an astonishingly detailed, nine-paragraph answer.

At some point in the proceedings, Anita decided to join the conversation to offer a few choice comments about Brian Jones. In the tiny leopard-skin bikini that was always her outfit of choice at Nellcôte, Anita looked good enough to make a dead man come. Unlike me, Keith remained so centered that not even Anita could distract him.

The session was so intense that when I finally turned off the tape recorder an hour and a half later, I felt as though I had just done a full day's work. When I asked Keith if we could do this again tomorrow at the same time and place, he said we could just pick it all right up from where we had left off whenever we next sat down to talk.

I then spent days waiting for this to happen. Fortunately for me, I happened to be living at Villa Nellcôte during what I would later come to call "the garden period." Because the only intoxicating substances being passed around on a regular basis were smoke and wine, every day seemed like an excuse for another party.

Depending on how Keith felt when he came downstairs in the morning, he might have someone bring around the motorboat so we could all go water-skiing in the bay. Or he might spend a few hours sitting in the sun on the back steps reading the day-old English newspapers that had just been delivered to the house. Lunch out on the patio was always a major production. What with all the fuming hash joints and bottles of ice-cold white wine being passed around the table, the meal would sometimes go on for hours.

Once it was over, Keith might want to go for a drive in his red Jaguar XK-E. Stopping at some deserted beach just before sunset, he was more than happy to spend half an hour skipping stones off the water so they bounced again and again before disappearing beneath the surface. The point being that if Keith was happy, then so was everyone else at Villa Nellcôte. Whatever he chose to do on any given day became the central activity in which everyone else wanted to be involved.

Actually knowing who all these people really were or what they were doing at Nellcôte turned out to be a question no one could answer. If Keith said someone was cool, nothing more needed to be asked about them. With the possible exception of Anita, the single most impressive-looking person in the house was

Tommy Weber, a long-haired race car driver who seemed to have stepped right out of the pages of F. Scott Fitzgerald's *Tender Is the Night*.

Tommy's two young and completely adorable sons, Jake and Charley, also known as "Boo-boo," were also there. This was a somewhat sad story because their mother, a beautiful young woman who called herself Ruby Tuesday, had only just taken her own life. Despite the fact that he was still mourning her loss, Tommy seemed to be having an extraordinary amount of fun at Nellcôte. One day he impressed everyone by telling us how he had just picked up a woman and then had it off with her on Errol Flynn's yacht, which was moored nearby.

And then there was Spanish Tony Sanchez. With his dark shirred hair and sharp-boned face, Tony, or "Spanish," as only Keith ever called him, would not have looked out of place selling stolen goods on some crowded street corner in Soho. Although Tony seemed a pleasant enough fellow, what I did not know then was that he was not just Keith and Anita's friend but also the long-standing dealer by appointment to the Rolling Stones.

Desperately in need of money some years later, Tony would write a scurrilous and curiously inaccurate book about his drug-filled days and nights with Brian Jones, Marianne Faithfull, Keith Richards, Anita Pallenberg, and Mick Jagger. By then, Tony's time of service with the Stones was long since over. And although Keith so terrified the man while standing beside him at a urinal in a club in London one night that Tony actually pissed on himself, he somehow managed to pass away some years later in a remarkably peaceful manner.

Accompanying Tony at Nellcôte was his girlfriend, Madeleine. Despite never having very much to say, she also seemed quite nice.

Two years after her stay in the South of France, Madeleine would be turning tricks in Brighton for fifteen quid a night to support her heroin habit. She would later be found dead by her close friend Marianne Faithfull.

Wearing a full white racing suit adorned with a Grand Prix emblem, Keith's good friend Stash also came to stay for a while at Nellcôte. Born Stanislaus Klossowski de Rola in Switzerland, Stash had attended an English boarding school, become an actor, and then played in a band that had opened for the Rolling Stones at the Olympia in Paris in 1964. As I later learned, he was the son of Balthus, the world-famous painter of prepubescent girls whose genius as an artist apparently included imagining himself to be a count, which may have explained why Stash liked to refer to himself as the heir apparent to the long-defunct Polish throne.

It was not just the complete lack of pertinent background information concerning my fellow residents at Nellcôte that kept me in the dark about them. The rhythm of daily life in the house was so removed from ordinary reality that I was completely oblivious to much of what was actually going on around me. All I could really think about was when I would get to talk to Keith again.

Fueled by tequila, a libation no one I knew in England was then drinking on a regular basis, my second interview session with Keith took place right after lunch a few days later. While we were talking to one another, our conversation seemed utterly brilliant to me. When I played back the tape later that afternoon, I realized that the gaps between my questions and Keith's answers kept increasing in direct proportion to our continuing intake of tequila. By the end of the interview, the two of us were communicating in monosyllabic grunts that would have made no sense whatsoever on the printed page.

Despite how badly I needed to talk with him again, days passed without another session. Realizing that Keith was not about to sit down with me again until he was good and ready, I stopped emerging from my room bright and early each morning with my tape recorder in my hand. On some level, I cannot say I was all that unhappy because in that house, the music never stopped.

On a daily basis, cartons of albums that had not yet been released on either side of the Atlantic were delivered to Villa Nellcôte and then stacked up beside a turntable on which classic old soul, the blues, George Jones, Merle Haggard, Buddy Holly, and Chuck Berry were always going around. Long before it became the rage, Keith was crazy about reggae. Over and over, he would play a song with an infectious beat called "Funky Jamaica" by the JA Horns that really knocked him out.

Since no one on the planet was ever going to tell Keith Richards what kind of music he was going to play in his own house, I forced myself to stay up later than everyone else one night so I could put James Taylor's *Mud Slide Slim and the Blue Horizon* on the stereo without being laughed at. As I was lying back against some cushions and listening to it in a far corner of the darkened living room, the back patio doors suddenly swung open and in came Keith.

Stooped over like a peasant gathering grain in a painting by Millet, he slowly began picking up the toys that Marlon had left scattered all over the living room floor during the day. In many ways, it was what any loving father would do before retiring for the night. Only as Keith performed this task, he happened to spy a rather large and distinctly ominous-looking capsule that was lying in plain view on the Persian carpet.

Whether it was a leaper, a creeper, a black beauty, or some consciousness-expanding psychedelic substance, I had no idea. But without breaking rhythm or even pausing to consider the consequences, Keith picked up the pill and popped it right into his mouth. Shooting me a cynical look that left no doubt as to what he thought of my current musical selection, Keith then kept right on moving up the stairs. Despite how hard-core I now knew the man could sometimes be, even I was not prepared for the performance Keith put on at lunch the next day.

Within the music business by this time, word had gotten out that the Stones were planning to tour America once they had finished recording their new album. Like moths to a flame, various rock 'n' roll entrepreneurs made it their business to journey to the South of France to offer their services in putting the tour together. Earlier in the month, David Geffen had done his best to persuade the Stones that no one was better suited for the job than him only to have Mick Jagger decide otherwise.

Seated across from Keith at lunch this day at Nellcôte, the candidate in question was Jon Taplin, a Princeton graduate who was then managing The Band and who would go on to become a well-known film producer. Although he seemed perfectly pleasant, not to mention a far more competent businessman than anyone who had ever taken the Stones out on tour before, something about him rubbed Keith the wrong way.

As Taplin began detailing precisely how he would handle the tour of America to a tableful of people, none of whom he had been introduced to by name, Keith looked decidedly bored. Reaching for his acoustic Gibson Hummingbird guitar adorned with tiny flowers and butterflies on the pick guard, Keith leaned his head in close to the strings to make sure they were properly tuned.

Over and over again all week long until it seemed like he was trying to hypnotize himself, Keith had been playing "The Jerk," a

Curtis Mayfield and the Impressions sound-alike that had been a big hit for Don Julian and the Larks on the Money label in 1964. With his eyes shut and his head cradled against the body of his guitar, Keith started strumming the song's basic riff while mouthing the lyrics to himself.

Although Taplin did his best to keep right on pitching, he soon realized that no man was a match for Keith Richards when he was in this particular mood. Knowing he was not going to get the deal, Taplin quickly left the house once lunch was over. As though he had never even been there, Keith just kept right on playing the song over and over again.

Against such a force of nature, I stood no chance at all. And so when several more days passed without Keith sitting down to talk to me again, I knew there was nothing I could do about it but wait. At Nellcôte, everyone else still seemed to be having a fine time. Unlike them, I had an interview to do with Keith. But no matter how hard I tried, I could not get him to cooperate with me. For me, what had been rock 'n' roll heaven had now become rock 'n' roll hell. Trapped in the ninth circle where only the very worst sinners could be found suffering for eternity, all I could do was wait.

CHAPTER FOURTEEN

VILLA NELLCÔTE II, JUNE 5–11, 1971

ALTHOUGH I COULD NOT LET IT SHOW, I was now just as frantic as I had been while driving that sports car to Nellcôte for the very first time. Back in London, my sister and her two friends, all of whom had just graduated from college and were on the grand tour of Europe, were staying in my flat. I was supposed to be there with them but instead I was stuck at Villa Nellcôte hoping that Keith Richards would remember I was still alive so he would grant me another audience.

Like clockwork every day, I called Andrew Bailey in London to tell him how far away I still was from completing an assignment that should have been long since done. Caked with dust outside the villa, my incredibly expensive French sports car sat baking in the blazing hot Mediterranean sun. By the time I finally gave it back, the rental bill would amount to more than I made in a year working for the magazine.

At some point, Keith and I did a third session together that was far more scattered than I would have liked. And then . . . nothing. For reasons known only to him, Keith had lost all interest in the project. Like the great fish that Hemingway's old man waited his entire life to catch, Keith had spit out the hook and was now running away from me at top speed through some deep and silent sea only he could plumb.

Between the two of us, everything was still cool and he was still nice to me. But in his mind, the interview was now a thing of the past. Because Keith thought it was something he had already done, I soon became part of the scenery. Like everyone else at Nellcôte, I was now staying there because I had no place else to go. Not that any of them shared my discontent. Because the villa was the center of the hip universe, there was nowhere else they would have rather been.

One day after everyone else had left the villa to accompany Keith and Anita somewhere I did not want to go, I walked into the living room only to discover Mick Jagger sitting at the piano. Telling him how glad I was to see him, I shook his hand and we began to talk. Although we had not seen one another since he had confronted me between shows in the dressing room at the Roundhouse, the subject never came up between us. And while Mick had married Bianca since I had last seen him, I was not about to discuss that particular topic with him either.

Slowly picking out a melody on the keys with one finger at a time, Mick asked me if I knew where Keith might be at the moment. When I explained that he and Anita had left the house a while ago along with everyone else, Mick sighed like the weight of the world was upon his shoulders and told me that the two of them were supposed to be working together that day.

Although the Rolling Stones had been in the South of France for two months, the mobile recording truck had only just arrived at Villa Nellcôte. As Keith had happily explained to me, the current plan was to record the new album right there in the basement of his very own house. What Keith did not mention was that he and Mick had yet to come up with a single new song. It was for this reason that Mick was now playing the role of the wounded child for all he was worth.

Although it had been years since Mick and Keith had shared a flat and it would have been impossible to imagine them living in the same house for more than a day, being in the South of France had served to increase the psychic distance between them. Because Keith did not approve on any level of the life that Mick was leading, their working relationship itself was now in danger.

Despite my heartfelt promise not to delve back into italics, I feel compelled to do so one last time in order to detail why all the simmering tension that Mick and Keith had kept under wraps during the English tour was now an everyday fact of life in the South of France. Although Bianca would later say that her marriage to Mick ended on their wedding day, that star-studded event had also put the final nail in the coffin of the personal relationship between Mick and Keith.

Although Keith and Anita had been together for four years, they had never felt the need to get married. In their view, this was something that only straight people did. Nor did they see Bianca as someone suited in any way whatsoever for the rock 'n' roll lifestyle they had shared with Mick and Marianne Faithfull. Adding yet more fuel to the fire, Mick had spent the month before his wedding undergoing Catholic instruction so he could marry Bianca in church after a civil service at which Keith had served as the best man.

For those who may doubt that Mick's wedding day marked the final parting of the ways between the two songwriters who were the heart and soul of the Rolling Stones, consider how Keith chose to deal with the event. After getting as high as possible and then grappling with the local chief of police outside of the council chambers where the civil ceremony was about to take place, Keith chose for reasons known only to him to sit on the bride's side of the aisle. And while he was the one who came up with the bright idea of getting a massive rock superstar jam going at the party to celebrate Mick and Bianca's nuptials, Keith then offered his ultimate judgment on the entire affair by passing out in the balcony before he could even step onstage to play.

By choosing to make Bianca his lawfully wedded wife, Mick had made it plain that he was now beginning yet another brand-new chapter in his life. Although Mick and Keith were still joined at the hip when it came to writing, recording, and performing with the Rolling Stones, they were now heading off in wildly different directions.

And so what I did not realize as I watched Mick Jagger sitting at the piano in the living room of Villa Nellcôte was that from this point on, nothing between him and Keith would ever again be as it had been before. As everyone would come to learn in time, the music itself was all that they now really had in common.

///

After spending an hour waiting in vain for Keith to return, Mick walked out the front door, got into his car, and drove back to the mansion where he was living with Bianca. Unlike him, I could not leave Nellcôte until I had found a way to make Keith sit down with me for one last session.

Going into complete panic mode after a few more days had passed without being able to make this happen, I called Marshall

Chess in London. Throwing myself on his mercy, I explained how badly things had been going for me at Nellcôte lately and told him that if Keith did not sit down to talk to me again, the *Rolling Stone* interview with him would never appear in the magazine because it would not exist.

Getting on the case as only he could, Marshall immediately flew to the South of France. After he and Keith had vanished behind closed doors for what I later learned was a prolonged sit-down, Marshall told me that I would have just as much time as I needed with Keith the next morning.

On what I still remember as a particularly lovely day in the South of France, Keith and Marshall and I sat down at a wooden table beneath some trees behind the house. As a hot breeze from the sea rustled through the leaves above our heads, tiny songbirds trilled lilting melodies in the fragrant sunshine. Taking one hit after another off a tightly rolled joint as we talked so that the sound of the match scraping against the side of the box in his hand rumbled like thunder into my microphone, Keith was just as good as his word. Once the session was over, I had no more questions to ask.

At long last I was done. I had my parole. Packing my bag as quickly as I could, I said goodbye to one and all and walked out the front door of Villa Nellcôte for what I thought was the very last time. As I began driving back to Cannes in a car that now looked as though I had left it parked in the middle of the Gobi Desert for the past few months, I realized I could not submit the interview until I had given Keith a chance to read it. Which meant that I would be going back to Nellcôte again.

CHAPTER FIFTEEN

VILLA EDEN, JUNE 12–18, 1971

IN THE APTLY NAMED VILLA EDEN IN CANNES, I found myself sharing a dark apartment on the bottom floor with Jerry Pompili, whom the Stones had brought over to the South of France to continue working for them after the English tour had ended. For reasons neither one of us understood, this otherwise very ordinary block of flats on rue de Campestre seemed to have come equipped with a never-ending supply of hot and cold running stewardesses, all of whom were willing to do anything they could to get closer to the Rolling Stones.

Setting myself up at a table in the front room, I began transcribing the cassettes I had brought with me from Nellcôte. Without using earphones or a foot pedal, I sat for hours listening to what Keith had said to make sure I got every word right. Never all that easy to understand under the best of circumstances, Keith was virtually impossible to comprehend when he began slurring his words in what has since come to be his characteristic manner of speaking.

After piling up as many single-spaced pages of transcript as I could, I would climb into the front seat of Jerry's redoubtable

VW van so we could get something to eat. Since he had already determined that St.-Tropez was the place to be, we found ourselves there on more than one occasion. Having been invited to a birthday party for a local deejay one evening, Jerry and I arrived at the very posh Hotel Byblos where Mick and Bianca had spent their wedding night together just a month before.

Befitting our status as two serious long-haired dudes who had been out on the road with the Rolling Stones, both of us were wearing faded jeans and dark blue denim work shirts. For want of a better term, call it the early seventies rock 'n' roll hippie cowboy look for guys who would not have known one end of a horse from the other if their lives depended on it. Although we were with a French woman who knew everyone in town and kept whispering incredible bits of gossip about them in my ear as they walked in the door, all the other guests just kept staring at Jerry and me like we were the original ugly Americans.

As the French woman quickly explained to me, this was simply because of how we were dressed. In St.-Tropez that summer, everyone was wearing worn military fatigues. Because it was "la mode," Jerry and I looked so out of place that people were wondering aloud whether we were on our way to "le rodeo."

Which was just the way it was back then in the South of France. As the Rolling Stones themselves soon learned, the locals were always either at your throat or at your feet. Speaking the language definitely helped as did having vast amounts of money to spend but the highest trump card in the deck was being as famous as, how you say, "les Rolling Stones."

And so when Mick and Bianca showed up that night, every eye in the room followed them as they made their way through the crowded room to our table so they could sit down with the only people they knew. While Bianca was dressed to the teeth, Mick just happened to be wearing a pair of faded jeans and the same kind of dark blue denim work shirt that Jerry and I had on.

Before the week was out in St.-Tropez, every last hip young thing in town was walking around in faded jeans and a dark blue denim work shirt. Was this an accident? A simple twist of fate? You decide. What I do know for certain is that none of them would have been caught dead in such an outfit before seeing Mick that night had convinced them all that there was now simply nothing hipper to be worn in the world.

After spending a week in the front room at Villa Eden pounding away on the lightweight portable typewriter I had brought with me from London, I finally finished what amounted to nearly one hundred pages of transcript. Sliding the original into a manila envelope along with the carbon copy, I made my way back to Nellcôte.

As always, the front door was unlocked. Because the Stones had started jamming until all hours of the night down in the basement, the house seemed unusually quiet. When I finally found Keith, he was standing in the dining room. Explaining that I needed him to go over the interview to make sure I had quoted him accurately, I handed him the transcript. That Keith could take out anything he did not want to see in print went without saying.

For the next thirty minutes, I stood there in silence watching Keith smoke one cigarette after another as he read each page of the transcript of the interview before flinging it across the table. For any writer, watching someone read what you have written is always a nightmare. When what you have written is about that person, the experience becomes ten times worse. Would Keith hate the interview? Would he ask me to tone down some of the very explicit language? Or would he just sadly shake his head and tell me it would be better for all concerned if the interview never saw the light of day?

Unable to ask him any of those questions, all I could do was stand there and wait. Coming at long last to the bottom of the final page, Keith tossed it aside. Squinting sideways at me through the cloud of cigarette smoke that always seemed to be hanging around his head, he said, "Yeah, man. I said it. Go on and print it."

And that was it. No corrections. No additions. No subtractions. Keith did not care what anybody might think about what he had said because insofar as he was concerned, it was all true. In that moment, Keith Richards let me know who he really was.

CHAPTER SIXTEEN

VILLA NELLCÔTE III, JUNE 19–NOVEMBER 30, 1971

AS I WOULD LATER LEARN, there were so many hidden dramas going on at Villa Nellcôte during the long and fateful summer when the Rolling Stones were recording *Exile on Main St.* in Keith Richards's incredibly hot and humid basement that no one person could have been aware of them all. And while nobody actually died during the making of the album, so many lives were irrevocably altered in the process that I now feel compelled to examine the human toll that was exacted.

Seated right beside producer Jimmy Miller in the mobile recording truck parked outside the villa, Andy Johns recorded every take the Stones did over the course of those five months. Tall and lean with long dark hair hanging to his shoulders and a fine-boned face, Andy was then just twenty-one years old and looked every inch like the rock star he had always wanted to become.

Following in his older brother Glyn's footsteps, Andy had begun his career by working as a "tape jockey" at Olympic Studios in London in 1967. Asked by Jimmy Miller to come join him at Stargroves where the Stones were recording tracks for *Sticky*

Fingers in April 1970, Andy got to see for the first time precisely what it was that Keith Richards did for the Rolling Stones.

As Andy Johns would later say, "They were doing 'Bitch,' but Keith was very late so they were playing it without him with Jagger on guitar and the song didn't sound very good at all. I walked out of the kitchen and Keith was sitting on the floor with no shoes on eating a bowl of cereal listening to what they were doing and giving them all funny looks. Then he said, 'Oy, Andy, give me that guitar.' He put on his clear Perspex guitar and kicked up the tempo and put just the right vibe on it and the song went from a laconic mess to being all about groove. Just instantly. As soon as Keith started playing, he transformed the song into what it was meant to be."

After being asked by Mick Jagger to do the final mixes on "Wild Horses" and "Dead Flowers," Andy began working with Eric Clapton on the follow-up album to the hugely successful *Layla* by Derek and the Dominos. Although Clapton had just made Andy coproducer of the new album as a twenty-first birthday present, he did not hesitate for a moment when Jimmy Miller called to offer him another job. "I just said, 'Look, Eric, I've got to go work with the Stones for a few weeks in the South of France. I'll be back.' And of course that was *Exile* and I wasn't back for a year."

Taking up residence with Bobby Keys and Jim Price in a villa about forty minutes from Nellcôte, Andy sat in the mobile truck listening as the Stones jammed aimlessly night after night trying to find a groove. "On 'Tumbling Dice,' we spent two or three weeks just trying to get the track right. It was a performance thing and there were times when those guys could really play badly and sound fucking terrible. I had about thirty or forty or fifty reels of tape, each an hour and a half long, on just that one song. Jimmy wanted to save it all because we had a feeling that they might not ever get a good take and we'd have to stitch something together with editing."

While recording the Rolling Stones had never been easy, working with them in the South of France proved far more difficult than even Andy Johns could ever have imagined. Now using heroin again, Keith would often leave in the middle of a session to go upstairs and put Marlon to bed and then not return because he had passed out in bed. While overdubbing a guitar part, Keith would "also sometimes play the intro and then be tacit for the first verse and never come back in again at all because he had nodded out while Jimmy and I just sat there letting the tape roll."

As Andy Johns soon discovered, the few inspired moments of brilliant creativity at Nellcôte were far outweighed by the never-ending tedium. "I had already snorted heroin a few times but it was during the recording of that album that I really started using because it was just so fucking boring most of the time and there was so much waiting around and it was so easy to get. Marseilles was just down the road and you could buy a big bag of very powerful China White for not a lot of money. I was dipping into that all the time and not really thinking about it. Then I had to go back to England and I wasn't going to take any of it with me on the plane. When I got there, I felt like I had a bad flu or something for a couple of days and it didn't dawn on me what was really going on until I figured out, 'Oh, this is what withdrawal is like. There's not much to this.'"

Returning to the South of France, Andy continued snorting heroin while working on the album. "Jim Price and I were back at our villa one night when Keith came over. I went into my bedroom to change my shirt and Keith was sitting there with a needle and spoon and I'd been brought up to think that was very inappropriate behavior. But I was along the path a little bit by now so I said, 'What are you doing?' And he said, 'Oh, do you want to do this too?' And I went, 'Yes. Okay.' And he went, 'Oh, this needle's fucked. It won't work. We'll go back to my place.'

"So we jumped in his car and drove all the way back to Nellcôte, and Keith took me downstairs and cooked something up, and he didn't inject it into the vein. He just skin-popped me. And went, 'Now you're a man.' Which, looking back on it, makes me think, *How adolescent of him.* And how adolescent of me. *Oh, I'll do this too.*"

Barely able to see straight, Andy then made his way back upstairs and was sitting in the mobile recording truck when Ian Stewart walked in. Having known Andy since he was fourteen years old, Stu took one look at him and said, "You've been hangin' out with Keith, haven't you? Oh dear, he's in trouble. I'm gonna tell your brother." "I just lied and said, 'Stu, no. Please don't. I haven't done anything.' But he had picked up on it right away.

"I didn't actually become a junkie until later on because I could never figure out how to make mainlining work. I was in a hotel room in London with Keith and Anita, who I think really enjoyed turning people on, and she said, 'Oh, sweetie, come with me,' and she took me in the bathroom and mainlined me. By the time I went to Jamaica with the Stones to record *Goats Head Soup,* I was a full-on, card-carrying junkie."

Call it collateral damage if you like, but the list of all those who were using heroin while spending time with the Rolling

Stones at Villa Nellcôte would fill more than a single page in any reporter's notebook. And while there are many who consider *Exile on Main St.* the greatest album the Stones ever made, I still cannot look back on that long hot summer in the South of France without thinking that the smell of death was all around me.

CHAPTER SEVENTEEN

LOS ANGELES, MARCH 24–25, 1972

FORCED TO LEAVE THE SOUTH OF FRANCE in the fall of 1971 as quickly as possible so as to avoid being thrown into jail by the local gendarmes on a variety of drug charges, the Rolling Stones had come to ground in Los Angeles, a city where they had always felt very much at home. Under incredible pressure to finish the new album so they could tour America, Mick and Keith had just spent the past four months working together in the studio as harmoniously as they ever had before.

Which did not mean the work itself had gone all that smoothly. As Andy Johns would later say, "We all traipsed off to Los Angeles and it was still a bit tedious but we were getting things done and then I started mixing and it was going slowly. Mick wanted me to work faster but I got four or five mixes done and then I told him I was going home for Christmas and I got the feeling I was not going to be asked back. Which was what happened and they started working with someone else.

"Jimmy Miller had me come back to LA to produce a solo album with Jim Price. We were out in Malibu and someone had just given me a hash cookie that had started to come on really strong and I don't like that kind of stuff anyway so I was sitting in my room paranoid as hell with the chair under the door handle so no one could come in and the phone rang and it was Jagger. Who then had to proceed to eat a little bit of humble pie without sounding like it. When I said, 'You didn't call to say hello. What is it?' he told me, 'Well, you know, those mixes of yours, we can't seem to beat them.'"

Along with Mick, Andy Johns went into Wally Heider's studio to begin mixing again only to decide that he preferred working at Sunset Sound. "Mick said, 'Here are the tapes. Just finish the fucking thing. You've got two days.' I already had four or five songs done so I just stayed there and ended up mixing two-thirds of the record in one huge great mammoth forty-eight-hour session."

Nevertheless, the mixing process was still not done. Two days before Marshall Chess was scheduled to fly to New York City to hand-deliver the masters to Atlantic Records so the album could be released before the Stones began their tour, Mick Jagger, Jimmy Miller, and Andy Johns were still driving themselves crazy trying to come up with the final version of *Exile on Main St.*

One year to the weekend after I had seen the Stones play the final two shows on their farewell tour of England, I left the house high on a twisting road overlooking Topanga Canyon where I had been living for the past three months to talk to Mick for an article about the new album and the upcoming tour that would not appear in *Rolling Stone* until nearly another month had passed.

Back then, Los Angeles was most definitely not the city it has since become. While you could still get anywhere you needed to go on the freeway in twenty minutes no matter when you left your house or in which direction you were headed, the maleficent spirit of Charlie Manson was not yet entirely dead. Without warning up in those hot, dry canyons, things could suddenly get weirder than hell and often did.

This was also the era when the "Riot House" (aka the Hyatt House) on the Sunset Strip was filled with English music business heavies whose accents gave them total license to get just as crazy as they liked without ever having to suffer the consequences. However, even for those at the very top of the food chain in rock 'n' roll, actually trying to live in Los Angeles back then could induce a form of culture shock so severe that the only cure for it was to go back home again just as quickly as possible.

As Rose Millar would later say, "Mick Taylor and Chloe and I moved into this house on Stone Canyon Road just up a bit from Keith and Anita and it was awful and I couldn't stand it. There was this concrete log in the fireplace and everything was white and made of plastic. Even in January it seemed like summer and what saved our lives was the Edwin Hawkins Singers doing 'Oh Happy Day.' Both Mick and I loved that song so much and every morning we'd wake up and say, 'Oh no, we're still here,' and put on the song and go back under the bedclothes. I thought LA was much worse than the South of France because there was so much cocaine around and that was when Mick Taylor began doing it in excess."

Authentically depressed by his new surroundings as well as by the glacial pace at which work on the album was proceeding, Mick Taylor had begun writing notes about how he no longer wanted to be in the Rolling Stones. Taylor had also told the young woman who was taking care of his daughter just how lonely he felt because he never got to meet anyone anymore. For someone stuck in Los Angeles without enough to do to occupy his time, it was not an atypical reaction.

Not surprisingly, this was not the way Mick Jagger felt about Los Angeles. For starters, he had set himself up with Bianca and their five-month-old daughter Jade in a huge southern California Gothic mansion on St. Pierre Road in Bel Air. Originally built for *Tarzan* star Johnny Weissmuller with an artificial waterfall that had long since gone dry, the house was surrounded by thickets of tangled vines and dense underbrush and looked as though it had come straight out of *Sunset Boulevard*.

On the Saturday I went to see him, Mick came padding barefoot down the sweeping staircase at four o'clock in the afternoon. Wearing a shiny silk zippered jacket with two tigers snarling at one another across the shoulders, he walked into the huge dining room and sat down at the table to talk to me with a beer in his hand.

As a sprinkler whispered softly outside the window, Mick began describing *Exile on Main St.* by saying, "It was cut during the summer and we'll be touring this summer, so it all fits in. It's a summer-y album and very commercial, I think. It's a double album like *Electric Ladyland*. God knows, there was enough in that for a year's listening."

Shifting his focus to the upcoming tour, Mick noted that the schedule was really not all that grueling. "It's like the one we did last time. Five cities a week for six weeks. We wanted to have rest in the middle, two weeks off to recover, but that meant we'd have been in the country more than six months and eligible for national service. You know, the draft."

The concept of Mick Jagger and Keith Richards being summoned to take their draft physicals so they could then be inducted into the United States Army and sent off to fight in Vietnam because the Rolling Stones had spent too much time in America was so completely ludicrous that I should have laughed out loud when Mick said this to me. Instead, I reported his words just as he had said them and his statement then ran in its entirety in *Rolling Stone.*

Continuing to make it all up as he went along, Mick talked about how he wanted to see the Stones begin experimenting onstage as they had done while making *Their Satanic Majesties Request.* "I mean," he said, "Mick Taylor has even more strange ideas than me and I know Charlie wouldn't mind going along with it. I wouldn't want us to be a band people think they could rely on."

With what I have now come to recognize as the kind of improvisational genius even the great Charlie Parker might have admired, Mick said the Stones would be doing "a little bus tour of the Deep South." He then expressed his desire to put on a concert in Los Angeles "outside in the open air, smoggy and all." That the Rolling Stones would not be doing any such thing until all the lawsuits still pending against the band for their ill-fated concert at Altamont had finally been laid to rest, Mick did not bother to say.

Although Mick did find it a bit annoying that movie star tourist buses had begun stopping outside the driveway of his house, he said, "The anonymity here is pretty good. It's not like England where it's so crowded that one has to buy a thousand acres to have any privacy and where they line up outside your house to find out who you fucked the night before. I hate that place. You think if only they'd let you, you could take it over and really get it together because it's so small really. You think that something like the miners' strike is going to really bring about a change. But it's such a pathetic little village sometimes."

Concerning his feelings about the country where the Rolling Stones were currently wanted by the police for questioning, Mick sighed and said, "Do you know there are no more salmon in the rivers of France? They've killed them all with pollution. In Nice and Cannes, the French are thieves. I'll never live there again."

After going upstairs to gather his things together so he could go to the studio, Mick walked back into the dining room and said, "People have asked me if I'm not frightened to go out onstage and work every night in America. Maybe you shouldn't even print anything about that. But, I mean, if we can't play here, in our other home so to speak, what good is it?" Knowing he had just delivered the perfect exit line, Mick then headed out the door.

After having driven down Sunset Boulevard in a big black Mercedes, Mick walked into the studio so he could make yet another attempt to come up with a final mix for the song that after much discussion he had already selected to be the first single from the new album.

As Andy Johns would later say, "We had recorded 'All Down the Line' at Nellcôte and then overdubbed it in Los Angeles. It was the first song that actually got finished, and Mick said, 'This is a single. This is a single!' And I thought, *He's out of his fucking mind. This is not a single.* So I said to him, 'You're wrong about this. This is not a single.' And he went, 'Really? Do ya think so?' And that was the first time I realized, 'Jesus, he'll actually listen to me.'

"I was having a hard time mixing it and I said, 'Jeez, I just can't imagine this on the radio.' And Mick said, 'Do you want to hear it on the radio?' And I said, 'Yeah. How do you . . . ,' and he said, 'Oh, we can do that.' And he went, 'Stu, call up that radio station. Go round there with the tape. We'll call you from the limo.

Have 'em put it on.'

"I was tooling up and down the Sunset Strip in the back of this limo with Keith and Mick and Charlie listening to a mix on the radio. I mean, how surreal is that? And Mick says, 'What do you think?' The sound system was so ratty in the limo that I said, 'I don't know, man.' And he said, 'We'll have Stu play it again.' Picking up the phone, he said, 'Stu, have 'em play that again.' Sure enough. There it was again. I thought that was pretty cool. But in the end, they decided 'Tumbling Dice' was the single."

Despite having made this decision, Mick still looked none too pleased as he walked through the control room door of studio number 3 at Wally Heider's that night. "Was this the Beach Boys' studio?" he asked. "I mean, I've been here before. You lose all the highs."

Hesitantly, the regular studio engineer, who would not be allowed to touch a single knob or dial that night, said, "Uh, actually it was completely rebuilt a while ago. You might still think there's too much bottom but that's because the top is going out over your head." Not at all happy with this answer, Mick grimaced and decided to just try to make the best of it.

Sitting alongside producer Jimmy Miller at the board, Andy Johns cued up a rough mix of "Tumbling Dice." From out of the speakers came a raging river of sound. Four guitars, two playing rhythm, one tracked through a Lesley, Bobby Keys on saxophone, Jim Price on trumpet and trombone, Nicky Hopkins on piano, Mick Taylor on bass, Charlie Watts on drums, Jimmy Miller on drums in the coda, and Clydie King and Venetta Fields on backup vocals. When the song finally ended, it seemed very quiet indeed in the room.

"Well," Andy Johns said. "What do you think?"

Looking up at the soundproof ceiling, Mick said, "I want the snares to crack and the voices to float. It's tricky all right. You think you've got the voices sussed and all of a sudden the backing track seems so. . . . " Stopping for a moment to find the proper word, Mick finally said, " . . . so . . . *ordinaire.*"

After rewinding the tape, Andy Johns began flicking knobs and turning dials so he could come up with a brand-new mix. Like magic, the bass guitar receded and the drums sounded crisp as the guitars began to overlap as they had not done before. Not at all certain that he liked this version any better than the last, Mick was suddenly distracted when Bianca walked into the room. Looking just as fabulous as ever, she sat down on the couch and began smoking a cigarette as Andy Johns rewound the tape yet again.

Even for Los Angeles back then, an awful lot of cocaine began going around the room. Since no one was going home anytime soon that night and the entire process was so laborious for those who had now been working on this album for nearly a year, it definitely seemed better to be wired than to fall asleep during the session.

After playing Mick yet another mix that did not seem to please him, Andy Johns said, "I thought you liked cymbals like that."

Shaking his head, Mick said, "They sound like dustbin lids."

Pouting for a moment, Andy Johns then began rewinding the tape so they could start all over again. And so it went until long after I had left the studio and gone back home.

That Keith Richards was nowhere to be seen in the studio that night spoke volumes about who was now running the show insofar as the new album was concerned. Whether this was because Mick was the one who always took over at this stage of the proceedings or because Keith had far more serious personal issues to deal with at the time was hard to say.

After having made my way up the very hip and fashionable Stone Canyon Road in Bel Air the next day, I found Keith lying on the roof of the big two-tone Chevrolet parked in front of his house making faces at his son Marlon through the windshield. Because Keith only ever existed in present time, our conversation began as though it had only been a few days since we had last seen one another at Villa Nellcôte. That we now both somehow found ourselves in Los Angeles was also of no great concern to him.

Climbing down from the roof of the car, Keith put out his hand and said, "Hallo. Have you heard? They're at it again. They decided to remix the whole album. Been up for thirty-one hours so far, I hear." Laughing, he said, "Always happens. The more you mix, the better it gets." Picking Marlon up in his arms, Keith then led me into the house where he had been living for the past four months.

Everything there was even more chaotic than usual because Keith and Anita were packing so they could board the four o'clock flight to Geneva the next day. Looking hugely pregnant, Anita walked past us into the kitchen. Explaining how this came about, Keith said, "We figured Marlon was lonesome so we let it happen." Asked if she was carrying twins, Anita sternly replied, "No, it is the dress." Without further ado, she then began throwing her belongings into the first of the nineteen pieces of luggage they planned to take with them the next day.

Sitting down at the table in his dining room just as Mick had done in his house, Keith began telling me how nice it had been for him to make the new album at Villa Nellcôte even though what with the band playing all night long in the blazing heat, things had gotten a bit hectic in the house. "But," he said, "with the truck always outside and ready, we could just go downstairs whenever we felt like it and work on a riff."

Concentrating on coloring circles on a piece of paper with a yellow crayon he had just found, Keith said, "I'm not even thinking about this tour. I'm just going to show up and be on it. I wish we'd work some places we haven't been like Kansas City. We've only been to Memphis once but that's because you get hung up in the same old circuit of cities all the time. We've got a short list of people we'd like to take with us. The Staple Singers or Joe Tex. An old bluesman would be nice but they're pretty fragile."

Asked if this would be the Stones' last tour, Keith suddenly looked up and said, "I doubt it. We need the money." Launching into full stream-of-consciousness mode, Keith then began talking about his recent fairly disastrous attempt to perform onstage in Los Angeles with Chuck Berry, how he had really wanted to release "Sweet Virginia" as an easy listening single, and what a gas it might be if the Stones decided to play a festival in Lebanon this summer.

Whatever he was about to say next was cut short by the sound of the phone ringing. After picking it up and listening for a moment, Keith mumbled something into the receiver and then hung it back up again. Looking at me like the real fun was about to begin, he said, "They've got the new mixes at Marshall's house. Let's go!"

In the little pool house up on Mulholland Drive where Marshall Chess was living within spitting distance of Jack Nicholson and Warren Beatty, the scene was fairly frantic. Chris O'Dell, who was now working for the Stones in Los Angeles and for whom

Leon Russell had written "Pisces Apple Lady," was on the phone looking for a piano player in case Mick decided he wanted to cut a promotional radio jingle for the new album.

More or less talking to the room at large, she said, "Billy Preston wasn't home. Stevie Wonder is available but I haven't asked Mick about him. I called Carole King and she said that what with the new baby and all, she wasn't working much anymore."

Looking as though they had both just been launched from a cannon at the circus, Jimmy Miller and Andy Johns charged in through the front door. Holding album sleeves in his hands, Miller said, "Take that shit off and play something good. We've redone five songs."

After the final chords of the brand-new mix of "Tumbling Dice" had faded away, Mick shut his eyes and said, "You know, Jimmy, they're both good."

"Maybe the old one," Keith mumbled.

"I think the new one is more commercial," Miller said.

The two mixes sounded so much alike that not even Mick could tell which one he had just heard. After a long discussion about the relative merits of each version, Keith asked which mix would sound better in mono. For a moment, no one said a word.

"Okay," Jimmy Miller conceded, "the old one. We'll go back now and play with it."

"Yeah," Andy Johns agreed. "Just a fraction more top on it. It's still a bit dull."

As they started collecting the mixes, Mick grabbed a piece of paper and began drawing the album title the way he wanted to see it appear on the cover. Talking to himself on the far side of the room, Marshall Chess said, "Fanatics." Laughing softly, he then repeated the word far more emphatically than before. Ten months after they had first begun recording at Villa Nellcôte in the South of France, the new Rolling Stones album was finally done.

With the sun fading behind the hills and the light failing outside the windows of the little pool house, Mick and Keith sat slumped side by side on a couch in the middle of the living room. In the gathering gloom, all you could see were their pale white faces and dark feathered hair. For what may have been the last time in their lives, they looked like brothers.

CHAPTER EIGHTEEN

VANCOUVER, JUNE 3, 1972–
NEW YORK CITY, JULY 26, 1972

WHILE I CERTAINLY ENJOYED MYSELF on the Rolling Stones 1972 tour of America, the tour itself was most definitely not fun. Rather, it was a military campaign of the first order, a rock 'n' roll version of General Sherman's March to the Sea that enabled the Stones to cross over into a brand-new market that would continue to expand exponentially with each passing year.

In terms of the zeitgeist, the tour was precisely what the age demanded. Over the top, loud, violent, angry, decadent, and incredibly lucrative, it bore no resemblance whatsoever to the extremely civilized cakewalk I had experienced with the Stones in England just fifteen months earlier. The real miracle was that I even managed to get myself on the tour in the first place.

Despite all the time I had spent with the band over the course of the previous year, I discovered to my great shock that I was not the fair-haired boy at *Rolling Stone* that I had imagined myself to be. And so I had to call in as many favors as I could from those who worked for the Stones before the magazine agreed to let me cover the tour. Although I also wanted to write a book about the tour, the man who ran the magazine's publishing division simply could not have been less interested in the idea.

Even though I had to put my great dream of becoming a published author on hold, the good news for me far outweighed the bad. At long last, I was going to get to write about something big. Exactly how big, I had no idea until I began hanging out at the Beverly Rodeo Hotel in Los Angeles where the bar was always filled with hookers and tour manager Peter Rudge, Jo Bergman, Alan Dunn, and Chris O'Dell were frantically working to put together shows by the Rolling Stones in thirty-two cities over the course of the next fifty-three days.

Unlike my account of the English tour which had focused solely on the Stones and their offstage adventures, what I wanted to do this time around was cut back and forth between the band, the supporting musicians, the people working on the tour at every level, and all the insanely obsessed fans who were willing to go to impossible lengths just to see a single show.

What I did not realize until the tour actually began was that in order to do this I would find myself spending just as much time outside the awful hockey arenas where the Stones performed as I did backstage with the band. As I soon learned, the hordes of angry kids who assembled out there each night had not come to hear the music but rather to do some fighting in the street.

And so instead of helping Keith Richards break into a locked dressing room, as I had done on the English tour, I found myself hanging alongside Peter Rudge on a large corrugated metal door that forty kids without tickets had already managed to lift four feet off the ground at the Pacific Coliseum in Vancouver so they could come rushing in for free.

In Seattle, I watched Mick Jagger walk toward the band's private plane with a blond girl who might have been twenty years old. In a plain cotton dress with no makeup on her face, she would not have looked out of place selling cookies and lemonade at a high school dance. After bidding her goodbye, Mick looked at me with a lascivious grin on his face and said, "Yeah, I had a nice bit of sex last night. Know what I mean?"

Why Mick had even gone to the trouble of telling me this, I had no idea. No more than five minutes later, he was clutching the armrest of his seat in abject fear while explaining that the power turn the Stones' private jet was now making was the single most dangerous moment in any flight. As always, it was just Mick being Mick. On the road in America, I soon learned there was no way of knowing what he might say or do in any given situation.

Unlike the English tour when I had been the only reporter traveling with the band, the Stones were now accompanied from city to city by a press contingent so large that it would not have looked out of place on a presidential campaign. To protect Mick from physical harm and ensure that Keith would not get busted for drugs by local cops, they were both surrounded by several concentric circles of heavy-duty security. Unless you were doing heroin, there were also certain rooms into which you simply could not go once the show was over. Despite these constraints, certain moments that occurred while I was out on the road with the Stones that summer have stayed with me ever since.

After visiting Dealey Plaza so I could look up at the sixth-floor window in the Texas School Book Depository from which the Warren Commission claimed that a lone gunman had assassinated John F. Kennedy, I found myself drinking dark beer and eating pizza with Charlie Watts late one night in a very collegiate bar in Dallas. Delighted not to be recognized by anyone, Charlie stared at his food and said, "It's not much of a way to see the country, is it? All you care about is how the bed is and can you get something to eat after the show?"

Before the show in Houston the next night, I was banging away on my portable typewriter in the little trailer the Stones used to leave the arena each night when Charlie stuck his head in through the window. After watching me for a moment, he said, "Doin' your homework then, are you?" With his drumsticks spinning like helicopter rotors in his hands, he then walked out onstage to play.

In New Orleans, Ahmet Ertegun threw what must still rank as the greatest party I have ever attended in my life. As Roosevelt Sykes, a sixty-six-year-old Chicago-based boogie-woogie piano player known as "The Honeydripper," Snooks Eaglin, a blind guitarist, and the fabled Professor Longhair performed, people danced themselves into a daze in a room where the temperature was easily 100 degrees. When a New Orleans street band began strutting across the floor led by a magnificent old black man in a black hat and white gloves with a starred white sash across his chest and a stuffed pigeon dangling off one shoulder, everyone began walking behind them in time to the second line while waving white handkerchiefs in the air.

In Mobile, Alabama, I saw what I still believe to have been a moment of authentic social change in America when an audience comprised mainly of white kids got on their feet to dance as Stevie Wonder, who opened so brilliantly for the Stones each night, launched into "Superstition." Once the show was over, Ian Stewart, who would log an astonishing 8,000 miles in rental cars before the tour was over and then sleep for three straight days on the ocean liner taking him back to England, drove me at top speed through Biloxi, Gulfport, and Bay St. Louis in Mississippi on Highway 90.

By the time my first article appeared in *Rolling Stone,* I had already been ordered to leave the tour. Whether this decision was based on how much money the magazine was spending to keep me on the road, the quality of my writing, or the fact that *Rolling Stone* had also decided to have Truman Capote write his own account of what it was like to journey through America with the Rolling Stones, I had no idea either then or now.

All I knew was that Truman was in and I was out. Leaving the tour at its midway point in Nashville, I flew back to Los Angeles and began cranking out what was to be my final massive report about the Stones at play in Hugh Hefner's Playboy Mansion in Chicago, the incredible saga of Cynthia Sagittarius, the twenty-one-year-old hippie girl who hitchhiked to every city on the tour and then just waited outside the hall until someone gave her a ticket, and how it felt to be surrounded by thick-necked cops in the Deep South who hated everyone and everything having to do with the Rolling Stones.

After having filed reams and reams of copy, I was horrified to see that all my deathless prose had been slashed to ribbons. Thoroughly overwrought, I called the editor at the magazine who had sworn on a stack of Bibles that I would be allowed to cover the entire tour. The moment he got on the line, I began lecturing him about how you just could not lie to people in this world and then ever expect them to believe you again. On and on I went, telling him in no uncertain terms just how wrong what he had done really was. And then, without further ado, I told him I was quitting and slammed the phone down as hard as I could before he could say another word.

It was not until a few days later that I realized just how badly I had screwed up. Not only was I no longer on the tour, I had also just walked away from the only job I had ever loved. Not yet twenty-six years old, I knew my career as a writer was over. Because going to school was the only thing I was good at, I decided to try to enroll at UCLA for a PhD in English. Exactly what I was going to do with this degree if and when I ever completed my studies, I had no idea.

And then a letter arrived that had been forwarded to me from the magazine. Having read what I had written about the Stones, the man who ran a publishing house that has long since gone out of business and had been named after a magazine that also no longer exists asked me if I would be interested in writing a book about the tour.

Rushing to the phone, I called him in his office in lower Manhattan, negotiated what seemed to me like the truly fabulous advance of $3,500, and flew to New York City in time to catch the final four shows of the tour at Madison Square Garden. After checking into a hotel across the street from the hall that made the Black Hole of Calcutta seem luxurious by comparison, I went backstage with my bright red tour laminate in hand so I could watch the Stones perform for the first time in nearly a month.

What with Truman Capote and Andy Warhol sitting side by side like a pair of elder vampires in the Stones' dressing room and every star-fucker in town doing all they could to get as close to the band as possible, the backstage scene at the Garden was a human zoo.

When I had last spoken to Mick as he sat in a hotel room in St. Louis watching the Democratic convention on television with the sound turned, off, he had told me that the shows in Madison Square Garden were going to be something special. Hyping the event as only he could, Mick had said, "Maybe I'll stand on my head, pull off all my clothing, and just go crazy. Hopefully, by that time, I'll be completely mad."

Literally reduced to skin and bone by the physical nature of his performances night after night as well as by the vast amounts of cocaine nearly everyone on the tour had been doing to keep themselves going, Mick seemed so wired in New York that he could barely answer an interviewer's question without jittering in place like someone had inserted a live wire into his spine.

With dark shadows beneath his eyes and the skin drawn so tightly against the bones of his face that he seemed to be wearing a mask, Keith Richards looked no better than Mick. Being Keith, he did come up with my favorite line of the tour at the madhouse of a press reception that followed the first show at the Garden. After being told by some woman he did not know just how good he had been in some movie she did not name as well as how much she wanted to thank him for what he had given her, Keith turned to me with a completely deadpan expression on his face and said, "I never fucked her. I swear."

Accurately describing the insanity that the Stones had generated in New York, Keith looked around the room and said, "Right now is when you realize you're a product." In terms of what the gods of commerce had done to the holy grail of rock 'n' roll, no truer words had ever been spoken. For me personally, the end of the tour was so truly sad and thoroughly disheartening that after the final show in Madison Square Garden on July 26, 1972, I never saw the band perform onstage again.

At the time, all I really cared about was that I finally had a book to write that someone actually wanted to publish. To gather the material for what would become *S.T.P.: A Journey Through America with the Rolling Stones,* I spent the next three months interviewing everyone who would speak to me about what had really happened behind all those closed hotel room doors during the long hot summer when the Rolling Stones had journeyed through America on what to that point in time was the highest-grossing tour in the history of rock 'n' roll.

CHAPTER NINETEEN

KINGSTON, JAMAICA, DECEMBER 1972

ALTHOUGH KEITH RICHARDS DUG THE FUNKY VIBE so much that he promptly bought the mountaintop estate overlooking Cutlass Bay that had once belonged to British pop star Tommy Steele, the Rolling Stones had not come to Jamaica to record their new album because of all the beautiful beaches that dotted the island or to avail themselves of the plenteous supply of ganja that Bob Marley would soon make famous all over the world. Simply, the Rolling Stones had come to Jamaica because they had nowhere else to go.

In Kingston, where the band was staying in the sprawling mansion that had been the home of Island Records founder Chris Blackwell before being converted into the Terra Nova Hotel, the gun culture still ruled the streets. Outbreaks of political violence by warring gangs fighting to control the drug trade were the rule rather than the exception. Without all the security that had accompanied them on the American tour, the Stones were now isolated, beleaguered, and very much on their own.

Although the rich, thick smell of flowers filled the air in Kingston, the huge turkey vultures known on the island as "john crows," that came swooping over the swimming pool at the Terra Nova each day, seemed like harbingers of evil. When Bill Wyman's female companion was raped in their hotel room by an intruder who forced Wyman to hide under the bed during the attack, it only served to confirm that the Stones were now surrounded by a kind of darkness they had not known before.

Stateless and homeless, the band was now truly in exile as they had never been in the South of France. The psychic toll exacted by this condition was so exhausting that it began wearing on the Stones in ways even they could never have explained. You could hear it in the music. In Jamaica, the overall feeling was so grim that on every level it felt like the end of the line.

What should have been a simple nightly trip to Byron Lee's Dynamic Sounds recording studio at 15 Bell Road on the edge of Trench Town instead became a military expedition of the first order. As soon as the van that had brought the band from the hotel pulled to a stop outside the studio, everyone filed as quickly as possible down a narrow alley to a door where two heavily armed guards stood watch. Once all the musicians were inside a studio where the walls were pocked with bullet holes, the doors were locked for the night and no one went outside again until the session was over.

Despite how awful the decision to record their new album in Jamaica now seemed, the Stones were also besieged by a sizable portion of the English rock press as well as a host of Japanese reporters and photographers who had come to file stories about the band's upcoming tour of the Far East. So near yet so far away, the press corps would all sit by the hotel pool each morning literally twitching with envy as they stared at the nearby table where the Stones and their people were having breakfast.

For me, Kingston was the final stop on what had seemed like a never-ending research trip. During the past three months, I had spoken with Hugh Hefner in the living room of the fabled Playboy Mansion in Beverly Hills and listened to Bill Graham tell fabulous stories with the timing of a Borscht Belt comedian in his home in Mill Valley. I had interviewed Truman Capote in his home overlooking the sea at the tip of Long Island and gotten to meet the great director Elia Kazan, who was then living with Peter Rudge's ex-wife in Manhattan. In Boston, Mayor Kevin White, a true old school politico, had begun talking before I could even turn on my tape recorder about the night he had walked out onstage to beg a sold-out crowd to be patient while they waited for Mick and Keith to be released from a Rhode Island jail.

In London, I had actually persuaded Ian Stewart to sit down with me for one of the few interviews he had ever done in his life. I had also spent a memorable day riding through Hertfordshire swilling Courvoisier out of plastic cups with Bobby Keys in the back of a long black limousine as he went looking for a place to live in the English countryside.

In the middle of the afternoon, Bobby and I found ourselves sitting in a very grand and rather stuffy living room across from Barbara Cartland. Despite the fact that the overly made-up seventy-one-year-old woman known as the queen of the romance novel most certainly did not need the money, she happened to have a cottage for rent.

"And so, young man," the future Dame Commander of the

British Empire trilled in her impossibly upper-class accent while looking right at Bobby, "what is it exactly that you do?"

While my best answer to her question would have been "running wild while doing whatever he pleases on tours with the Rolling Stones," this was not how Bobby Keys dealt with her inquiry.

Like a true son of Texas, Bobby politely explained that he was a musician who specialized in playing the saxophone. Because I knew who Barbara Cartland was and Bobby had no idea whatsoever, the entire scene seemed like something out of a Restoration comedy. And while she did offer him the cottage, Bobby wisely decided to continue looking elsewhere for his very own rural rock star retreat.

After returning to New York City, I had flown to Kingston, checked into the Terra Nova, and begun interviewing all those I had not seen since the tour had ended. My task was complicated by the fact that as always when they were in the studio, the Stones were working throughout the night and then sleeping all day long. After several failed attempts to talk to Mick, I finally left a note on the door of his room asking him to give me a call.

When I answered my phone at some ungodly hour of the night, I was so asleep that Mick just laughed and said it would be better if we spoke to one another at a more convenient time. As good as his word, he sat down with me for a lengthy interview. Making everything yet more difficult, all the Rolling Stones except Keith then flew to France to appear at a hearing in Nice on drug charges stemming from the summer they had spent recording at Nellcôte.

For the Stones, the stakes were very high indeed. If the French authorities decided to issue an international warrant for Keith's arrest, the band's tour of the Far East would have to be canceled. As Keith would later say, "It's all a bunch of political bullshit. . . . I have the feeling the French are trying to show the Americans that they are doing something about the drug problem. But rather than actually doing something about it, they bust a big name. The only thing I resent is that they try and drag my old lady into it. I find that particularly distasteful."

With no one left for me to interview, I checked out of the Terra Nova and went to visit an English rock photographer who was spending two years in Port Antonio teaching at a local school. At one point during the utterly terrifying train ride through the Blue Mountains, a woman at the back of the car held up her young son so he could piss a glittering yellow stream down the aisle. For the rest of the ride, I watched the pool of liquid slosh back and forth between the seats as we rounded one treacherous turn after another.

After arriving in Port Antonio, I learned there was a reggae show that night at the local cinema featuring Toots and the May-tals and Desmond Dekker. Although I really wanted to see them perform, the rock photographer informed me that because several people had been hacked to death with machetes at the last reggae show there, this would not be a good idea. Which was just how wild it was in Jamaica back then.

Although the hearing in Nice went well for the Stones with all of the witnesses testifying they had been browbeaten by the police into filing false statements, an arrest warrant on charges of drug trafficking was filed against both Keith and Anita in France. Returning to Kingston, the Stones then spent another two weeks in the studio without getting very much done. And while Bill Wyman would later write that producer Jimmy Miller collapsed and engineer Andy Johns became ill in Jamaica, the truth was that along with Keith, they were all so strung out on smack that working on the new album did not seem nearly as important to them as finding a way to stay high.

As Andy Johns would later say, "By the time we went to Jamaica to do *Goats Head Soup,* my habit had gotten pretty serious. Keith, Jimmy Miller, and I were the junkies and we ran out of stuff so someone flew in and tightened us up. Then Jimmy said, 'Fuck this. I've got enough left to make a trip back to LA and cop for us all.' While he was gone, Keith and I were going through withdrawal like mad and then Keith called up and said, 'I bet Jimmy left something in his bathroom.'

"So I got assigned to break into Jimmy's room. Maybe we even had the key. I went in and the first place I looked was in his electric razor. Bingo, there were a couple of grams. I came out of the room and Keith said, 'Oh great, I'll have that.' And I said, 'What are you fucking talking about? Fair dues.' He could be really naughty like that. So we split it and then we ran out again and I was upstairs in my room and it was so bad that I could not even have the sheets touch me.

"It was that uncomfortable and Keith called and said, 'Oh, we can drink our way through this. Come on down to the bar and have some drinks with me.' I went down there and he was fine. I took a sip of a Bloody Mary and threw up. Looking back on it, Keith had obviously gotten something from somewhere and just wanted someone to hang out with and he didn't share any of it with me."

Because they were still "junk buddies," Andy Johns remained close to Keith even after the Stones left Jamaica on December 13, 1972 without having achieved very much at all in the studio. In June 1973, both Keith and Anita were busted in Keith's house on Cheyne Walk for grass, Mandrax, and heroin as well as a collection of burnt spoons and syringes.

Far more seriously in England, Keith was also charged with possession of unlicensed firearms and ammunition, specifically a .38 caliber Smith & Wesson revolver he had bought for $200 from one of his black security guards on the American tour and then taken with him to Jamaica for protection, 110 rounds of ammunition, and a 9-millimeter Belgian shotgun with a sawn-off barrel that all by itself would have landed him an automatic sentence of a year in jail.

As Andy Johns would later say, "Keith was up for what was probably the worst bust he'd had so far. When the coppers walked into his bedroom on Cheyne Walk, he had immediately grabbed three or four blackened spoons and started stirring this old cup of coffee to get the smack off them and the detective inspector went, 'You don't have to bother with that. We've already got you.'"

Clad in a black chalk stripe suit and a white shirt with no tie, Keith emerged from his limousine outside the Great Marlborough Street Magistrates Court in London on the day of his hearing with an unlit cigarette dangling from one corner of his mouth. Looking every inch like a glamorous movie star queen, Anita was decked out in a floppy hat, her best jewelry, and a sheer black blouse through which her breasts were clearly visible.

Despite the way they looked, Keith was so concerned about the possible outcome of the hearing that he had spent the previous week hanging out with Andy Johns. "This was Keith's second or third bust," Andy Johns would later say, "and it really looked like he was going to go down. To distract him, I had taken Keith to Hamleys, the big toy store in London, and we'd gotten all these models to build just to keep his mind off of things.

"On the day of the trial, I got to lower court and I had been up for two or three days and I smelled just rank. I remember sitting in the back of the courtroom with Mick Jagger on one side of me and this woman from the *Daily Express* on the other with my arms clamped firmly to the sides of my body so this awful pong didn't come out too much. I said to Mick, 'What's going to happen?' And he said, 'I think Keith's going down. But it's all right. I've got Jesse Ed Davis with his bags packed in LA. He can be on the next plane.' Which I thought was beyond mercenary. Because they had to tour with *Goats Head Soup* which was just about to be released.

"The prosecutor read out this list of twenty-five charges and I thought, *Well, he's sunk. That's it.* But then Keith's barrister got up and said, 'Mr. Richards obviously could not have been residing at Cheyne Walk. Otherwise, he would have been liable for a million pounds in tax.' Then they presented all these letters from various people saying that some roadie had left the firearms and the ammo in the house. The barrister said Marshall Chess had been living there and Keith understood that Marshall had a drug problem but he had promised Keith he was straight now and so Keith felt very let down by him. It was very fucking naughty and they really did a number on Marshall. Boing! A 250 quid fine for Keith and Anita and off they both walked."

After Keith and Anita had made their way through all the press people gathered outside the courtroom, they slid into the backseat of the Daimler limousine where Andy Johns was waiting for them. "I had a gram of blow in each of my socks and I just handed one gram to the left and one to the right because I was sitting between them and off we went to the Londonderry Hotel to celebrate Keith's release.

"We were all sitting there and feeling shitty and waiting for the man and all the kids were in the next room. Marlon and Dandelion Richards and my son William, who was then still quite young. They were all sleeping on this bed and sure enough, one of them had knocked over a lamp and set fire to the mattress. The smoke filled up this teeny little annex corridor and then started coming into our room and everyone panicked.

"Fortunately, I had this bag from Biba's so I went in the bathroom and filled it up with a water a couple of times and put out the fire. And I thought, *Fuck, Keith has only just gotten off three hours ago and here we are again. Doesn't take much time.* I knew I had to get out of there and as I was jumping in the elevator, the hotel manager was coming the other way and all the people on the floor were saying, 'Lock him up. Throw the key away. He's endangering our lives.'"

Although Keith somehow managed to talk his way out of the situation, he was banned from ever staying again at the Londonderry Hotel. "There had been a fire while we had been recording at Nellcôte and then Keith's house in Sussex had burned down as did Mick Taylor's house during that period. Wherever he went back then, Keith was always followed by a trail of fire."

While Keith may have never known he was about to be replaced in the Rolling Stones by Jesse Ed Davis, a talented guitarist who would himself eventually die of a drug overdose, the fact that

Mick Jagger was ready to do this to keep the band on the road spoke volumes about how their relationship had changed over the past two years. Although neither of them knew it at the time, the writing was also on the wall for both Jimmy Miller and Andy Johns.

By the time the Rolling Stones went to Munich in 1974 to record *Black and Blue,* Miller had been replaced as the producer of the album by Mick and Keith, aka The Glimmer Twins. After showing up late for the first session because one of Keith's friends had stolen his stash and then subsisting for a while on heroin that Mick "was kind enough to steal from Keith for me," Andy Johns was told not to come back after the Christmas break. Neither he nor Jimmy Miller ever worked for the band again.

Despite how dire the scene in Jamaica had seemed, it soon became just another dark chapter in the never-ending story of the Rolling Stones. In time, both Mick Taylor and Bill Wyman would leave the band. For wildly different reasons, Jo Bergman, Marshall Chess, Chip Monck, and Peter Rudge would also soon be gone.

In 1985, Ian Stewart would die of a massive heart attack at the age of forty-seven while sitting in his doctor's waiting room. After doing a show in his memory at the 100 Club on Oxford Street, the Stones would go right on touring just as they always had done before. In time, Mick and Bianca would part company as would Keith and Anita but the Stones still soldiered on.

As their former manager Andrew Loog Oldham, whom the Stones had also left behind, wrote of them, "Stars must be killers, always striking first and last. . . . There's no remorse when they kill, no regrets when they pimp and no shame when they whore. And it's really a fair exchange: the world needs them and they need the world."

While some may view this as the devil's bargain, the truth was that Mick Jagger and Keith Richards simply could not survive without making music and then walking out onstage to perform before huge crowds all over the world. As everyone would learn over the course of the next five decades, it would never be over for the Rolling Stones until Mick and Keith were finally done.

HAIL AND FAREWELL

AFTER FINDING MYSELF A SMALL CABIN overlooking the ocean in northern California for the princely sum of $125 a month, I started working on the book that came to be entitled *S.T.P.: A Journey Through America with the Rolling Stones*. Sitting at a desk a carpenter friend had built for me, I wrote a chapter a week and then went out on Friday nights to celebrate.

The first full-length account ever written about a rock tour, the book has since been republished in America and the United Kingdom and remains in print to this day. Having said that, the reviews that greeted *S.T.P.* when it first appeared were most definitely mixed.

In *Rolling Stone* magazine, the late Chet Flippo wrote, "Greenfield is perhaps too much the objective observer, too much the disinterested journalist. He never explains why he was kicked off the tour, he never develops a coherent viewpoint. At different times, he appears as 'I,' as 'this writer,' and 'anyone.' Ultimately, *S.T.P.* is part of the endless coverage of the Stones, who . . . manage either to be substanceless people or project a public image of vacuity."

In *NME,* the weekly English music business trade paper, the late Mick Farren, the former lead singer of the Deviants who was himself no mean writer, noted, "I fear this book may be the one that could finally O.D. the reader on rock writing, particularly that flat, conscientious, detailed, post–Truman Capote style that has made *Rolling Stone* what it is today. . . . The book shows that writers like Greenfield can get locked in by rock and roll. Instead of wearing out his buns hanging around on a Stones tour, he should be with the real action."

To all these charges even at this late date, I do plead guilty, Your Honor. For the record, I should also like to state that when someone half my age recently asked me if there was anything left to say about the Rolling Stones, I said, "No." Which of course did not stop me from going on at length about them here for the third time in my career.

And now at long last, we come to the title of this book. As all dyed-in-the-wool fans of the band already know, it happens to be a line from "Angie," a song that Keith wrote while kicking heroin in Switzerland shortly after *Exile on Main St.* had finally been deemed ready to be delivered to Atlantic Records.

As Nick Kent, the mild-mannered English rock journalist who went into a phone booth in London one day only to reemerge as the second coming of Keith Richards, wrote in *NME* when "Angie" was released, "This is positively the most depressing task I've had to undertake as a rock writer. This single is a dire mistake on as many levels as you care to mention. 'Angie' is atrocious."

Although "Angie" ranked fifty-ninth in *Rolling Stone* magazine's list of the Stones' top one hundred songs and remains the only ballad by the band ever to go to number one on the charts while also featuring Mick Jagger's faintly audible guide track— also known as a "ghost vocal"—I cannot say I disagree with Nick Kent's appraisal of it.

As a song, "Angie" still seems pretty soppy and far too sweet for my taste but there you go. My original title for this book was *Goodbye, Johnny B. Goode* but after a good deal of discussion about whether anyone would know what this meant, the marketing director at Da Capo Press came up with *Ain't It Time We Said Goodbye* and I decided to go with that instead. Having said this, I am really glad I did.

After lo these many years, the time has indeed finally come for me to say goodbye to the band without whom my career, not to mention my life, would have been radically different in so many ways. Perhaps because I walked before they made me run, I have nothing but positive memories of the time I spent with the Rolling Stones.

On every level, the pleasure was definitely all mine, and I would not have wanted to miss any of it for the world. Or as Keith wrote to Mick Taylor after learning he had left the Rolling Stones, "Thanks for all the turn-ons."

ACKNOWLEDGMENTS

FIRST AND FOREMOST, I would like to thank Ben Schafer, my editor of long standing at Da Capo Press and fellow aficionado of beatnik literature, who gave me the go-ahead to write this book. My thanks also go to Kevin Hanover who came up with a title that I liked more than my own.

As always, I would like to thank all those who were kind enough to make the time to speak to me concerning the Rolling Stones' 1971 tour of Great Britain. In alphabetical order, they are Lady Elizabeth Anson, Jeff Dexter, Alan Dunn, Chip Monck, Noel Monk, David Noffsinger, Jerry Pompili, Jim Price, Jeff Stacy, and Tony Smith.

For his invaluable help in finding information about The Big Apple in Brighton, I would like to thank Robert Allan. For helping me sort out exactly what happened in Belfast in the spring of 1971, my thanks to Joe Stevens.

For being a lifelong pal and going through his archives for me, I would like to thank Phil Franks, whose excellent website, the Philm Freax Digital Archive, is a treasure trove of information about the underground scene in England during the early 1970s.

For providing me with the wonderful photograph of Ian Stewart and Mick Jagger, I would like to thank Will Nash. Anyone interested in his remarkable book about Ian Stewart can contact

Will at info@out-take.co.uk. I would also like to thank the great Chip Monck for providing me with photographs from his own extensive archive.

For directing me to the *Daily Mirror* archive, where I was astonished to find a photograph of myself from the 1971 tour I had never seen before, my thanks to Adam Cooper. David Scripps at the Mirrorpix Archive made it possible for me to use these photographs in this book. Thanks as well to Peter Everard Smith for the photo of the Stones performing at the Roundhouse in London that graces the cover of this book.

Closer to home, I would like to thank Chris Cochran, who kept me working through his computer magic. For their friendship and never-ending support, I would like to thank Jeffrey Greenberg, Paul Goldman, and Janice and Brian Higgins.

My gratitude for all they did for me goes to Dr. David Dansky, the incredible human heavy metal beat box machine also known as Dr. Scott Smith, Dr. Jeremy Silk, Ryan Vereker, and all the nurses and incredibly caring staff at the Community Hospital of the Monterey Peninsula.

As always, I could not have written this book without Donna, and I thank her for sticking with me through some truly hard times. I should also like to send special love to Sandy and Anna.

If you will permit me, I should like to add one final thought. Whether we know it or not, we are all closing by secondary intention. Along the way, the least we can do is try to shed some light on the process.

SOURCES

MUCH OF WHAT APPEARS IN THIS BOOK comes from the two spiral-bound notebooks I filled during the 1971 Stones farewell tour of Great Britain. I have also drawn on interviews I conducted in the past with Marshall Chess, Andy Johns, Glyn Johns, Astrid Lundstrom, Rose Millar, and Keith Richards.

ARTICLES

Robert Greenfield, "The Rolling Stones on Tour: Goodbye Great Britain," *Rolling Stone,* April 15, 1971.

Robert Greenfield, "Keith Richard: The *Rolling Stone* Interview," *Rolling Stone,* August 19, 1971.

Robert Greenfield, "The Rolling Stones in LA: Main Street Exiles," *Rolling Stone,* April 27, 1972.

BOOKS

Julian Dawson, *And on Piano . . . Nicky Hopkins: The Extraordinary Life of Rock's Greatest Session Man.* San Francisco: Backstage Press, 2011.

Pete Fornatale, with Bernard M. Corbett and Peter Thomas Fornatale, *50 Licks: Myths and Stories from Half a Century of the Rolling Stones.* New York: Bloomsbury, 2013.

Robert Greenfield, *S.T.P.: A Journey Through America with the Rolling Stones.* New York: E. P. Dutton, 1974.

Robert Greenfield, *Exile on Main St.: A Season in Hell with the Rolling Stones.* New York: Da Capo Press, 2006.

Bill Janovitz, *Rocks Off: 50 Tracks That Tell the Story of the Rolling Stones.* New York: St. Martin's Press, 2013.

Bobby Keys, with Bill Ditenhafer, *Every Night's a Saturday Night: The Rock 'n' Roll Life of Legendary Sax Man Bobby Keys.* Berkeley, CA: Counterpoint, 2012.

Lisa A. Lewis, ed., *The Adoring Audience.* London: Routledge, 1992.

Prince Rupert Loewenstein, *A Prince Among Stones: That Business with the Rolling Stones and Other Adventures.* New York: Bloomsbury Press, 2013.

Will Nash, *Stu.* London: Out-Take Limited, 2003.

Philip Norman, *Mick Jagger.* New York: Ecco Press, 2012.

Andrew Loog Oldham, *Stoned: A Memoir of London in the 1960s.* New York: St. Martin's Press, 2001.

Keith Richards, with James Fox, *Life.* New York: Little, Brown and Co., 2011.

Dominique Tarlé, *EXILE: The Making of* Exile on Main St. Guildford, UK: Genesis Press, 2001.

Bill Wyman, with Richard Havers, *Rolling with the Stones.* New York: DK Publishing, 2002.

FILMS

Charlie Is My Darling: Ireland 1965, produced by Andrew Loog Oldham, photographed, edited, and directed by Peter Whitehead. ABKCO Films, 1966.

Crossfire Hurricane, written and directed by Brett Morgen. Eagle Rock Entertainment, 2012.

Gimme Shelter, directed by Albert Maysles, David Maysles, and Charlotte Zwerin. Maysles Films, 1970.

WEBSITE SOURCE

Robin Millar, "Rose and the Stones," available at: http://www.robin millar.org.uk/autobiography/rose_stones.htm.